Discover your Ancestors

Discover Your Ancestors' Occupations

Laura Berry

Discover Your Ancestors' Occupations

First published in 2015
Discover Your Ancestors Publishing
www.discoveryourancestors.co.uk

Printed and bound in Great Britain by Acorn Web Offset, Wakefield

A catalogue record for this book is available from the British Library

ISBN 978-1-911166-02-3

Written by Laura Berry
Edited by Andrew Chapman

Design: Prepare to Publish Ltd

Contents

Introduction

For family historians, an ancestor's occupation is often the most intriguing aspect of their life. It's one of the first details we learn about an individual from civil registration certificates and census returns, and it defines the person we imagine them to have been. On seeing their job title we make assumptions about their social standing, culture, the characters they would have mixed with, and their financial means. Did they live comfortably or was life a struggle? Did their toil and hard work result in you leading a better life today? It's fascinating to map a family's changing fortunes, but of course it's not always a happy story.

An ancestor who threw caution to the wind and broke the mould often captures the imagination. There's a huge appeal about a person who had the guts to take a risk and do 'something a bit different', whether or not they succeeded. The 1891–1911 censuses tell us whether our ancestor was a worker, an employer, or working on their 'own account', meaning self-employed. This way you might discover that they set themselves up in business. Perhaps that entrepreneurial spirit is a family trait. Actors are often keen to know whether they were the first person in their family to tread the boards; or could it be an instinct that runs through the genes, passed down from a previous generation?

Whether you're descended from a long line of thespians, greengrocers or railway labourers, there's much to learn from exploring occupational records. People spent most of their lives earning a crust, especially before the introduction of old-age pensions in 1908. Until 1944 the majority left school well before the age of 15 to start contributing to the family income, a fact that is reflected in the censuses available every 10 years from 1841 to 1911, where you'll find the occupations of everybody in the household listed.

Your ancestor's employment may have taken them away from the family home, which could explain why you have struggled to find them living with loved ones. For example, ten-year-old Henry Eaden appears on the 1841 Windsor census in the household of his employer James Hastings, who was a chimney sweep. The census entry for Henry (see overleaf) lists his occupation as 'chimney sweeper journeyman' – 'journeyman' was a term that was applied to lots of different types of craftsmen who had served an apprenticeship and mastered their art, but who still worked for another member of the trade rather than on their own account.

5

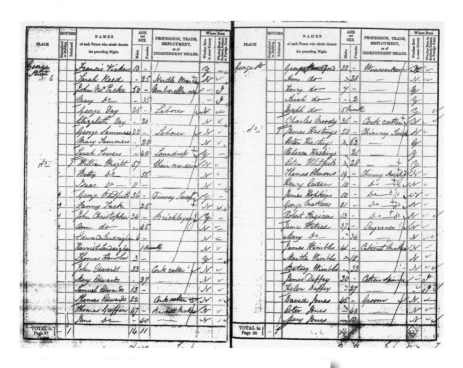

Census image and transcripts for Henry Eaden at www.TheGenealogist.co.uk, giving details of his occupation

Many old occupations can be quite baffling to us, since they died out generations ago. The industrial revolution created new roles just as quickly as it made others redundant through the mechanisation of production processes. Rural and skilled artisans employed in cottage industries, such as 'croppers' who sheared and finished woollen cloth, were increasingly forced to take up lesser-paid unskilled posts in mills and factories throughout the late 18th and early 19th centuries. Positions for 'shearing machinists' emerged, for instance, whereby a single person was needed to operate a machine that performed the work of four croppers.

There are various reference books for interpreting archaic words associated with the workplace, including Colin Waters' *A Dictionary of Old Trades, Titles and Occupations* (2002), listing everything from an 'abra' (maid servant) to a 'zythepsarist' (brewer), and *The Book of English Trades and Library of The Useful Arts*, dating from the early 19th century, which can be read for free online at **www.archive.org/details/ bookenglishtrad00soutgoog**. The section on weavers in this old book gives an interesting overview of how different types of weaving were performed to make silk, wool, linen and cotton cloths.

A weaver depicted in The Book of English Trades

Technological advances had surprisingly far-reaching consequences well beyond the start of the industrial revolution. In 1881, 72-year-old Charles Lingford of Bowling near Bradford was described as a former agricultural labourer but now a 'knocker up', a job that gradually disappeared in the early 20th century as more affordable and reliable alarm clocks reduced the need for a person to rap on workers' doors at dawn. Quite how the knocker-upper awoke on time each day is a mystery.

'Knocker up' Charles Lingford in the 1881 census

It's worth bearing in mind that certain unusual job titles had different regional meanings – for example a wherryman could be another word for a drayman, who drove a flat dray vehicle used for transporting heavy loads, but in areas where there were canals and inland waterways the wherryman might have performed a similar job to a bargeman. Joseph Wright's six-volume *English Dialect Dictionary* (1898–1905) comes in handy for such conundrums and can also be found online at **archive.org**.

By 1851 more people were living in towns than in the countryside in England and Wales, and the numbers of agricultural labourers and farm servants gradually fell over the coming decades from over a million to just 635,000 in 1911, by which time the effects of the long agricultural depression that started in the 1870s were acutely felt. The 1881 Census Report counted 1.3 million people as belonging to the agricultural class compared to 6.3 million in the industrial class. By 1891, when the population of England and Wales was recorded at 33 million, half a million were coal miners, a fraction of them pit lasses, a quarter of a million were clerks, and around 600,000 men described themselves as general labourers, more likely to be working on roads and building sites than in the fields.

There were 1.4 million women employed as domestic servants in the 5.4 million households recorded on the 1891 census, plus 100,000 as charwomen hired to clean, in comparison to 416,000 who worked as dressmakers and milliners. Perhaps worryingly for the welfare of the population, just 19,000 people were listed as surgeons, GPs and physicians (a third more were tobacconists), and 193,000 were in the teaching profession. You can find out how popular your ancestor's profession was by browsing tables of census statistics at **www.histpop.org**.

To a certain extent a person's choice of occupation was determined by where they lived. Perhaps they had little choice at all. Starting work at a young age meant that most people were sent to an employer by their parents, guardian, local authority or institution if they were in care. It's no surprise that generation after generation of my Yorkshire forebears went down the pit, and the sparsity of employment options in the area became starkly apparent when the collieries and steelworks closed in the 1970s and 80s. Just as at the start of the industrial revolution, the decision for the main breadwinner to move the family to another county or even another country at any point in time could have been influenced by a desire to change jobs or a need to find employment during a slump in the local economy.

You can start to track the peaks and troughs in your ancestor's career by looking for them in parish registers and ordering birth, marriage and death certificates, which will help to fill in some of the gaps between census returns.

It was common for people to supplement their income with more than one trade. For example, Samuel Meadows' children's marriage certificates described him as an excise officer, but their baptism records from the 1820s indicated that he also worked interchangeably as a shoemaker.

Social history books about the localities and the industries in which our ancestors worked may help to establish the reasons behind any dramatic changes in circumstances. The opening of a railway line might explain a sudden move across the country. Branches of my Yorkshire family were drawn down south during the 1920s when unemployment was high and the Kent coalfields were expanding. If things were really tough then a family might have been forced to seek relief from the Poor Law authorities, and the records of Boards of Guardians can give quite detailed explanations about why a family was in need. Another source of information are the registers of 'friendly societies', to which some workers paid a regular subscription as an insurance to cover them during difficult spells of unemployment, illness or injury.

Your ancestor's job could have ultimately led to their demise. Death certificates reveal tragic accidents in the workplace, which were frighteningly common before safety standards gradually improved in the lead up to the Health and Safety at Work Act, finally passed in 1974. However, long-term exposure to harmful substances also made people susceptible to terminal illnesses. Workers in the match-making industry, and others exposed to white phosphorus vapours, were at risk of developing phossy or fossy jaw. A hellish bout of toothache would degenerate into a putrid abscess, which not only caused disfigurement but could also lead to brain damage and organ failure as the jaw bone rotted away. In 1888 the London matchgirls went on strike over their disgraceful working conditions at Bryant and May's factory, but it took another 18 years for the substance to be internationally banned from production.

It's not always apparent that an ancestor died from an occupation-related illness, and careful research into the cause of death registered on a certificate may be required. For example, dressmakers were particularly prone to lung disease as a result of spending long hours breathing in fine particles of dust and fibres. In fact the incidence of 'phthisis' and 'silicosis' as causes of death on many certificates may be attributable to various different lines of employment, from mining to masonry work. Definitions of a large number of outdated medical terms can be searched at www.archaicmedicalterms.com.

Once you have created a timeline of a person's career using the basic family history sources, then it's time to dig deeper using a diverse range of occupational records, not all of which are available online. You may find that things are not quite as they appear. Delving deeper into staff registers could reveal that the man you had believed to be a respectable police constable on census returns actually had a rather chequered career.

Names of employers are sometimes given on the 1911 census, which is hugely useful for locating any detailed employment records, particularly for those in public service. One 68-year-old Ralph Vincent of Purley was a solicitor, but the 1911 census, which requested more detailed employment information than ever before, states that in addition to his freelance work Mr Vincent was a clerk and solicitor to Leyton Urban

Details of Ralph Vincent's employment in the 1911 census

District Council. It's possible that papers written in his hand will be found within the records of that council kept at Waltham Forest Archives.

You can also look at Ordnance Survey maps from around the turn of the century to try to identify exactly where your ancestor's place of work was and how far they had to travel. The censuses from 1901 indicate whether or not a person worked from home. There's a free selection of historical OS Maps online at **www.oldmapsonline.org** and more information about using a wide variety of maps to research employment history in the coming chapters.

This book takes a look at digital records and also some of the more unusual documents available in archives for ancestors who worked in agriculture, trade and industry, the professional classes and the entertainment sector. Going further, we'll look at living history museums where all the family can get a flavour of life as a Victorian workhouse master or blacksmith, as well as some of the courses out there for you to try your hand at your ancestor's trade.

EXPLORING OCCUPATIONS ONLINE

TheGenealogist.co.uk has one of the largest collections of occupation-specific records, from actors to teachers. And here are a few useful tips for occupational research using other tools at the site:

- The Person Search feature has a keyword box where you can type in an occupation, if this is already known, to help identify the right person.
- In census results (available for 1841 to 1911), clicking a person's occupation in the transcript brings up a full explanation of the job title, sometimes including what tools he would have used in his trade.
- The meanings of many old job titles can also be searched directly by keyword at **www.thegenealogist.co.uk/search/advanced/miscellaneous/occupation**.
- Middle class and artisan communities in some districts were drawn to Nonconformist chapels, and the records of ceremonies performed there can be found at the site, listing members' occupations between and before the censuses.

Exploring your family's connection with the landscape is a rewarding task

Chapter One: Agriculture

Deep research into the lives of ancestors who worked in agriculture is often overlooked, yet it is one of the richest areas of the family tree. If your rural roots were planted in one village for generations, then exploring your family's connection with the landscape is an especially rewarding task.

Agriculture played an important economic role even after the mills and factories of the industrial revolution punctured the British landscape, since the burgeoning urban workforce needed feeding. The agricultural revolution was curtailed in the early 19th century, having gathered momentum from the mid-17th century when technological innovation started to improve yields. A long agricultural depression resulted in civil unrest in the 1830s, and another ensued from the 1870s when it became cheaper for customers to buy imported grain. Some farmers adapted by converting from arable farming to livestock or dairy farming, but British agriculture has struggled ever since, despite support for homegrown produce during two world wars. Unpicking the impact that these events had on the lives of ordinary agricultural folk in your family can make for a fascinating journey.

Agricultural communities were built upon a traditional social structure that remained intact for centuries. Rural landowners employed a range of workers to maximise agricultural output. A steward might be employed to manage the workforce with help from a bailiff. Farmers were assisted by shepherds, cowmen and horsemen (a term that could encompass waggoners, carters and ploughmen), who ranked above the other labourers. Agricultural labourers lived in cottages with their families and often commanded better money than farm servants employed on short contracts to live on the farm and be available as and when needed. Jonathan Brown's book *Tracing Your Rural Ancestors: A Guide for Family Historians* (2011) provides a comprehensive overview of agricultural society from the bottom up. Women and children contributed significantly to a variety of tasks like harvesting, hoeing, weeding and planting, and so the whole family might be employed in agriculture at certain times of the year. Land records and the paper trail left behind by landowners often reveal more about the lives of these people, but are rarely indexed by name.

Feudal society

Archaeology has revealed that our ancestors began systematically farming the land over 6000 years ago when some of the first permanent settlements were established. None of us can hope to trace a line of descent back to the Iron Age, but, miraculously, surviving Saxon charters illustrate the ancient origins of some parish boundaries, delineated by hedges and ditches that are still maintained today. If you believe your ancestry goes back to a noble family in the 11th century then you might find mention of them in the Domesday Book recording lords of the land in 1086, two decades after William the Conqueror's barons set about seizing Anglo-Saxon estates following his victory at the Battle of Hastings. The Domesday Book has been translated from Latin and is searchable at **opendomesday.org**. Tenants-in-chief are also named, and descriptions are given of the agricultural holdings and the number of villagers, smallholders and 'slaves' or serfs working the land.

England and Wales's medieval feudal system was shaken by two catastrophic events in the 14th century – the Great Famine of 1315–1317, followed by the Black Death in 1348–1350, an epidemic that wiped out at least a quarter of the population. Consequently there was a labour shortage and the threat of another famine, encouraging workers to demand higher wages and serfs to break from their master's ties in search of better conditions elsewhere. Edward III's Statute of Labourers, passed in 1351, endeavoured to implement a wage cap and suppress the movement of peasants. It did however grant workers the right to offer themselves for hire at the nearest market town the day after Michaelmas at the end of September once the harvest was over.

Hiring fairs thus emerged as a regular event in the agricultural community's calendar. They persisted in some places until the late 19th and early 20th centuries, and their legacy remains in fun fairs held across the country. Men and women seeking employment stood in the centre of the market square with a token of their trade – a horseman's whip, a shepherd's crook, or a servant's mop. In Marlborough, Stratford-upon-Avon and elsewhere in the Midlands they are still known as 'mop fairs'. An employer might enter into a bond with the employee for as long as a year at these statute or 'stattie' fairs, as they were also known. Establishing the location of the nearest hiring fair to your ancestor's place of birth can be useful for understanding patterns of migration, since the fair might draw employers and job seekers from a 30-mile radius. At the height of their heyday in the 19th century the fairs were advertised in local newspapers, and where the market committee's minute books survive in the local archive they may provide lists of servants and their new masters.

Landlords have always needed to keep detailed administrative records for the effective management of their estates. Although parish records rarely exist before the 16th century, some estate records survive back beyond the 14th century and recall the community's sufferings during this tumultuous period. These documents, in varying states of decay, are usually in Latin before the early 18th century. Local history publications are therefore the best starting point for learning about the origins and early history of an agricultural community before tackling original records. The Victoria County History series offers a general overview of most English parishes, and a selection of volumes can be read online at **www.british-history.ac.uk/catalogue/secondary-texts**. These books invariably name the major landowners, shedding light on how estates have been subdivided over the centuries, not least during the Dissolution of the Monasteries from 1536 when the Crown acquired or sold off large tracts of church land to private owners.

Landed estates

The manor was the beating heart of rural life for many of our agricultural ancestors. Some manors comprised an entire village, or maybe even several hamlets and farms, while other villages were divided between various manors with numerous landowners. A manor might form part of a larger landed estate, which in itself could include several scattered manors under the ownership of a single lord. The lord of the manor was duty bound to hold a manorial court for his tenants, which prescribed the manor's customary rules and mostly dealt with matters of land, property and inheritance. The records of manors, and of landed estates that did not hold court, are full of references to agricultural workers of all levels.

The owners of landed estates took an increasingly 'hands off' approach from the 15th century, leasing out farms and property to tenants who took on the commercial risks and became responsible for all aspects of the operation, including hiring labourers. Whether or not there were tenant farmers, it was in the landlord's interest to keep regularly updated records. The archives of some estates can be found using the Manorial Documents Register at **discovery.nationalarchives.gov.uk/manor-search** and the National Register of Archives, which records the location of family estate papers at **discovery.nationalarchives.gov.uk/browse/c/Family/A**.

Many such collections contain estate plans showing the extent of the landowner's holdings at various points in time. This can be a useful starting point if you want to establish whether a farm where your ancestors lived formed part of a larger estate, in order to search for more paperwork. A variety of other maps and plans are also useful for this purpose and will be discussed shortly.

Depending on the size of the estate, there could be several levels of management responsible for record keeping. A steward might be supported in his work by a bailiff or reeve, ensuring that leases were issued to farmers and cottagers and their terms adhered to, that rent was collected where properties were let to workers, that the land was well managed, and both domestic and agricultural buildings kept in good repair. If you find an ancestor described as a bailiff or equivalent on the census then there's a good chance that you'll uncover correspondence written by him in the local archives.

The records they created were vast and varied, but fall into three principal categories: surveys, financial accounts and manorial court rolls. For a detailed explanation of the manorial system and the records it spawned, see Mary Ellis, *Using Manorial Records* (1997). Surveys generally describe the estate's holdings, and sometimes name tenants old and new where the survey was updated over time. Financial accounts might include rent rolls, accounts, tenancy agreements, leases, deeds and other ephemera showing how much tenants paid for their property, when they came and went, and whether they increased or reduced their holdings.

The Exbury estate book held at Hampshire Archives, for example, contains detailed information dating from 1718 to 1819 about various farms on the Mitford family's land, including a plan and summary lease for Stone Farm granted to tenant farmer Richard Bartholomew in 1731, which later passed to his son-in-law Charles Crumpe. This book was found simply by searching for Richard Bartholomew's name on the online catalogue at **http://calm.hants.gov.uk**, but the record is also indexed under the name of the farm and the estate.

Manorial court rolls are a complex but highly detailed set of records, which dealt in part with copyhold tenure peculiar to manorial estates. Every time a property passed to a new tenant, the old tenant needed to surrender the property before the manorial court and the new tenant had to be officially submitted onto the court rolls. The new tenant was given a copy of the court roll as proof of the transaction, hence the name 'copyhold'.

THE COURT ROLLS OF TOOTING
BECK MANOR.

Roll I.

December 13. 1394. The first Court of Dom Robert
of Wyndesore, Prior of Mertone, held there with view
of frank pledge, on the morrow of S'. Lucy the Virgin,
in the eighteenth year of the reign of King Richard
the Second, after the Conquest, Dom William Odiham
being Cellarer of Mertone.

i.
Totyngbek

John ate Grene	Thomas Haldone
Richard Jamys	William Brygthe
Richard Tobbynge	Richard Hamond
John Pykstone	Nicholas Cook
Richard Brygthe	John Brygthe
Walter Archure	John Spencere
John Morgone	Richard Brodwatere
John at Hethe	Thomas Craft

Fealty

All these did fealty to the lord and acknowledged that
they held from him as below.

Richard Jamys came to this court and acknowledged
that he held from the lord one tenement and 10 acres
of land, paying therefor 9ᵈ a year as fixed rent, and
for day-works in part commuted, 2ˢ a year. And he
further acknowledged that he owes to mow and lift
one acre and 3 roods of meadow. And he shall have
breakfast the first day. And he owes to reap in
autumn with one man for 8 days. And he shall be
at the lord's table at dinner and supper. And he
owes to weed the lord's grain with one man for one
day without food; and he owes to plough for one day
at the winter sowing and for one day at the Lent sowing

Fixed rent 9ᵈ

Release of
day-works 2ˢ

Customary
tenant

TheGenealogist.co.uk has a selection of early court rolls that have been translated from Latin, including the roll for the Manor of Tooting Beck, which was a rural area before it morphed with a string of neighbouring villages into South London's sprawling suburbs. The court roll of 1394 records that Richard Jamys held a tenement (dwelling) and 10 acres of land. The roll laid out in great detail the agricultural work that Richard was expected to undertake throughout the year, including mowing, reaping, weeding, ploughing and sowing. Furthermore, as a customary tenant, if Richard were to take a wife then he would owe the lord a cock and a hen at the festival of St Thomas the Apostle.

The manorial court also settled disputes between tenants involving small sums of money. Until land was enclosed (usually in the 18th–19th centuries) the court regulated cropping and the use of common pastures. The jurisdiction of manorial courts was gradually eroded away, and copyhold land ceased to be newly created from the 17th century. However, if your ancestors were copyhold tenants then they may appear in court rolls up to the early 20th century, and often properties passed from generation to generation. All remaining copyhold land was converted to leasehold or freehold following the Law of Property Act in 1922, and subsequently manorial courts were rarely held thereafter.

Although manorial holdings and landed estates in England and Wales were extensive, some agricultural properties have been freehold for longer than records will reveal. Most manors have been broken up bit by bit and former leasehold or copyhold farms and cottages have been sold with the freehold. Collections of sales particulars survive in local archives dating back to the 18th century and sometimes mention the name of the last tenant to live in the house.

A yeoman farmed his own land, but there is still the chance that the local record office could hold a farm diary or account book. Searching the local archive's online catalogue for the name of the farm and farmer can yield results, but it's always worth speaking to the archivist to find out whether there is additional material that hasn't been catalogued online. These men frequently left wills describing their property and who was to inherit it. They might even name servants who could be left small tokens of appreciation. See Chapter 5 for more information about locating wills.

The Museum of English Rural Life (MERL)'s archive in Reading has huge holdings of company accounts and farm workers' journals, including records of the Baylis family who farmed a large area of land in Berkshire and Hampshire in the early 20th century, covering Manor Farm, Eastbury, Bockhampton Farm and Leckhampstead Farm. The online catalogue can be searched at **www.reading.ac.uk/adlib/search/simple**.

Surveying the land

Identifying the location of the place where your ancestor lived and worked on old plans is not only useful for visualising the extent of the land they cultivated and visiting the fields today, but also for establishing whether it formed part of a larger estate to then search for estate records. A number of major land surveys from around the 18th century onwards are accompanied by written records listing the names of landowners and chief tenants, and also describe the land's use.

Enclosure plans and awards are the earliest of these, generated on a large scale from the mid-18th century when open fields were carved up, creating much of the patchwork of hedge-lined fields we see today. The enclosure of common lands, pastures and manorial wastes could be foisted on a rural community by wealthy landowners. Many smallholders and cottagers were allotted tiny plots of land in lieu of the loss of common rights. The enclosure award described the boundaries and identifying features of the newly enclosed plots, and the names of their owners. Maps were not always drawn up and are most common from the 1770s onwards, sometimes with a key showing who owned each plot.

TITHE RECORDS

The national collection of tithe apportionments and maps held at The National Archives has been exclusively digitised on **TheGenealogist.co.uk** where they can now be searched by name and parish. Digital copies of the tithe maps are linked to the apportionments so you can quickly see where your ancestor's land was.

To establish whether an enclosure award and map were created for your ancestor's parish, check the county-by-county indexes in W E Tate's *Domesday of English Enclosure Acts and Awards* (1978) and J Chapman's *Guide to Parliamentary Enclosures in Wales* (1992). Most maps and awards are held in local county record offices. For a detailed guide to enclosure records, see **www.nationalarchives.gov.uk/records/research-guides/ enclosure.htm** and Kain, Chapman and Oliver's *The Enclosure Maps of England and Wales, 1595–1918* (2004).

In 1836 the government passed a bill to convert all the tithes paid to clergymen by their parishioners from payments in kind (such as crops, milk and wool) to cash payments. Historically, tithes constituted a tenth percentage of the yearly profits arising from farming, which was due to rectors and vicars, or to 'lay rectors' where the right to the tithes had been sold to a private individual. When payments were made in kind the goods were stockpiled in large tithe barns; however, this was deemed impractical as time progressed. In order to establish how much money each person would need to pay instead, a national survey was made of all the parishes in England and Wales where a local Enclosure Act had not already commuted the tithes to money payments. Colourful maps of these parishes were drawn up over the course of the next 20 years and every plot of land was numbered. Accompanying tithe apportionments for each parish listed all the plot numbers, described whether they contained a house or other buildings, whether they were pasture, arable, meadow or garden ground, gave the total acreage of the holding and the names of the owners and principal occupant, and how much tithe rent was due.

John Hutchinson was described on his daughter's 1840 marriage certificate as a yeoman. This term could refer to farmers of large areas, but could equally apply to smallholders. The 1851 census on **TheGenealogist.co.uk** for Carlton le Moorland in Lincolnshire lists John as a 78-year-old 'cottager' of five acres, but turning to the 1849 tithe apportionment we gain a much fuller picture. This record set is uniquely

John Hutchinson's 1851 census and tithe apportionment records at TheGenealogist

available on TheGenealogist.co.uk, searchable by name and parish, and shows that John lived in a house with a garden and orchard amounting to one acre, which he rented from Mary Bradley. However he also owned three acres of pasture named Wheatley Close, where he could graze animals, and a smaller cottage and garden, which he rented to John Witherall. All of the plot numbers are given so that the exact position of these holdings can be pinpointed on the tithe map.

The next major national land survey was carried out shortly after Lloyd George's 1910 Finance Act proposed a new tax on the increase in the value of land resulting from expenditure of public money on local amenities. District valuers quickly got started surveying property in England and Wales, making enquiries about who owned and occupied each plot of land, including building plots, and assessing their value. They annotated Ordnance Survey maps with 'hereditament numbers' for each property – surviving working maps were transferred to local record offices and final copies were deposited at The National Archives. The hereditament numbers were noted into Valuation or Domesday Books deposited in local archives, recording the name of the owner and occupant, a description of the property and its value. Field books deposited at The National Archives in series IR 58 often give more elaborate written descriptions of buildings, their uses and state of repair, so you might discover that your ancestor had stables, cowsheds, or a pigsty in the garden, and that their house was in dire need of repair so perhaps times were tough. Their address on the 1911 census can be used as a starting point for the search, and there is detailed information about how to find the maps and field books at **www.nation-alarchives.gov.uk/records/research-guides/valuation-office-records.htm**. The survey was strongly opposed by landlords and the tax was never implemented, being repealed by the 1920 Finance Act.

Farmers were especially subjected to government scrutiny during World War Two since the nation relied on them for vast quantities of food while enemy attacks on shipping limited imports. War Agricultural Executive Committees were established in each county to rapidly increase the area of land under cultivation. A National Farm Survey was carried out between 1941 and 1943 to compile data about more than three-quarters of farms in England and Wales. The forms completed by the surveyors are now stored at The National Archives in series MAF 32, arranged by parish. They provide the name and address of the farmer, the number of labourers employed, how efficiently the farm was run and what was produced there. Just over half of the farms surveyed were run well, but a small fraction were badly managed, and occasionally the reasons for personal failings are given. For a detailed guide about how to access the records, see **www.nationalarchives.gov.uk/records/research-guides/farm-survey.htm**.

Questioning the status quo

The bulk of documents mentioned thus far are useful for researching ancestors involved in administration or who had some claim on the land, whether it be through ownership or a lease. Identifying itinerant labourers by name anywhere other than the usual family history sources is often an impossible task, but Ian Waller's book *My Ancestor was an Agricultural Labourer* (2007) greatly illuminates their lives. This poorly paid and ill-used class of workers gradually found a voice during the course of the 19th century.

Following a visit to the Wiltshire countryside in 1826, William Cobbett wrote of agricultural labourers that "dogs, hogs and horses are treated with more civility". The 1830s witnessed a spate of actions by labourers against their unprotected working conditions as rural unemployment worsened during the economic depression. In 1830 a fictitious character named Captain Swing issued threatening letters to employers who invested in threshing machines, reducing the availability of seasonal threshing work. Angry labourers across the south of England, who were generally paid less than their northern counterparts, rioted and deliber-ately damaged machinery. In many areas the Swing Riots were quashed by the militia and criminal charges brought against suspects. Jill Chambers's extensive research into machine breakers from across the country can be purchased in the form of books and CDs from **www.genfair.co.uk/supplier.php?sid=82**.

You have a good chance of identifying a labourer in court records, whether they were accused of rebellious acts or petty crimes like poaching. Migration in search of work may have taken your ancestor a short distance over a county border, so you may need to search for them in more than one record office. One group of farm workers from Tolpuddle, Dorset, formed the Friendly Society of Agricultural Labourers in 1834 to protest against cuts to pay. Six leaders including labourer George Loveless gained notoriety as the Tolpuddle Martyrs after they were charged with having taken an illegal secret oath and sentenced to transportation to Australia. The immediate aftermath of George's arrest in 1834 and subsequent pardon several years later is recorded in scanned transportation records on **TheGenealogist.co.uk**.

The Speenhamland system of outdoor poor relief supplemented labourers' meager wages in some parts of the country from the 1790s, but this came to an end with the New Poor Law in 1834. The Parliamentary Select Committee on Labourers' Wages had found in 1824 that the Speenhamland system was being abused and transcripts of evidence presented by men who worked with labourers can be read online at **http://tinyurl.com/pf6ljau**, including a list of all the labourers in Wilden, Bedfordshire. Parliamentary committees throughout the 19th century

George Loveless' records of transportation and subsequent pardon

highlighted the terrible plight of the agricultural poor, and their reports with first-hand evidence from labourers can be found at the British Library, The National Archives and numerous smaller libraries. The Royal Commission into the Operation of the Poor Laws, established in 1832, was particularly detailed in its contemporary accounts, as were Royal Commissions on Labour. Women and children who had worked in 'gangs' testified to having been worked to the bone for barely any remuneration. Labourers in remote areas of Northumberland complained that the bondage system still in effect in there meant an entire family was expected to work for a pittance in return for their accommodation.

'Friendly societies' were established to collect subscriptions for the welfare of members in times of need, and numerous trade unions emerged to campaign for better pay and conditions. The MERL archive hosts a large number of union archives, including accounts and minute books of the National Union of Agricultural and Allied Workers, and minutes of the National Union of Farmers established in 1908. Many of the larger trade unions had regional branches whose records are more likely to be deposited in the local archive.

There were a number of journals published in support of the upsurge in labour movements, which are useful for building up a picture of local working conditions. The National Farm Labourers' Union published the *National Agricultural Labourers' Chronicle* and Industrial Review (1875–1877), *The English Labourers' Chronicle* (1877–1894) was the official organ of the National Agricultural Labourers' Union; and *The Land Worker* voiced the concerns of the National Agricultural Labourers and Rural Workers Union from 1919. These and various other titles can be consulted at the British Library, where provincial newspapers reporting on village matters, local convictions, plough competitions and the like can also be read.

Broadening the picture

The most enjoyable part of discovering your ancestor's agricultural heritage is to get out there and explore the landscape where they worked. A trip to the countryside will be even more rewarding armed with the documentation already listed. With any luck the buildings, field patterns and tracks seen in historic maps still survive. Locating copies of old paintings and photographs of the area is useful for seeing how much or little the area has changed. Local archives are usually the best place for this, but there is also a growing number of historic images of villages online, including the Image Archive at **www.thegenealogist.co.uk/imagearchive/**.

Since many rural workers resided in small close-knit communities, it's worth investigating what material the local history society has collected. Books such as George Ewart Evans's Suffolk farming tales collected in the 1950s and 60s cast a light onto the vibrant fabric of agricultural society. The Royal Agricultural Society of England in Warwickshire is home to a large library of books (its historical membership records are kept at the MERL archive in Reading), and The Perkins Agricultural Library at Southampton University is another specialist repository for secondary sources.

If your ancestor's bucolic environment has been obliterated by modern development, there's still the chance to experience life in their shoes by visiting the Museum of English Rural Life in Reading, which has displays of agricultural implements and fascinating oral history accounts, or St Fagan's National History Museum celebrating country life in Wales through reconstructed historic buildings. There may also be a museum in your ancestor's home county, such as the Museum of East Anglian Life and the Kent Life rural heritage experience. These attractions also explore the lives of craftspeople and country traders, who are the subject of the next chapter.

IMAGE ARCHIVE

Find old photos of the villages and fields where your ancestors worked by searching for a place name or using the subject filters on **TheGenealogist.co.uk** Image Archive.

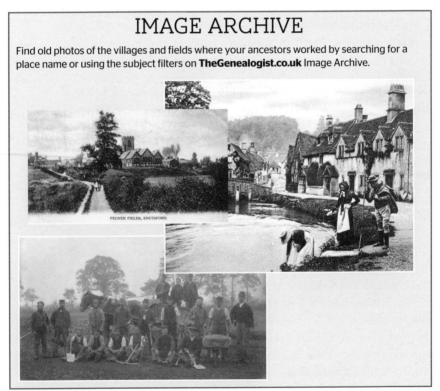

PEOVER FIELDS, KNUTSFORD.

Chapter Two:
Craftsmen, Tradesmen
& Merchants

The market towns across England and Wales were hives of economic activity and home to the burgeoning bourgeoisie. They particularly thrived during the 18th century when transportation improved along turnpike roads and canals. Craftsmen and women, artisans and merchants catered for the needs of an increasingly consumerist society, but it wasn't just townies who earned a crust from trading. The village blacksmith, baker, saddler and cobbler formed part of the fabric of rural society. Women could find employment in shops, perhaps assisting or even managing a family-run business. Such people were often well known within their community, so local history books for the town or village where your ancestors lived are a good starting point, since they often draw on memories, pictures and material collected from long-standing residents that may not even be found in an archive.

Guilds

Merchant and craft guilds emerged during the Middle Ages to control standards and prices, but also to support members during old age and times of need. Members of the same trade grouped together and paid for the administration of the guild to represent their interests nationally and in local government. Many city guilds persist to the present day, such as the York Butchers' Gild (sic). Merchants' guilds in particular tended to attract wealthy and influential members who played prominent roles in civic life.

People could join a guild or livery company by serving an apprenticeship (see below), or by 'redemption' (paying a fee) and invitation by existing members, or through patrimony if their parent was already a member. This way, women could bestow their father's membership to their husband or sons. Most guilds kept membership records listing places of birth and other biographical details. Sheffield Records Online for example has a database of masters belonging to the Company of Cutlers in Hallamshire, and also their apprentices at **www.sheffieldrecordsonline.org.uk/index_cutlers.html**. The records of guilds can usually be found in local archives, or if the guild is still in existence it may have a private archive. The Worshipful Company of Goldsmiths holds its court minutes back to the 14th century at Goldsmith's Hall in London (www.thegoldsmiths.co.uk/library/archives/). Guild members had an obligation to uphold the standards of their profession, and fines were imposed for shoddy workmanship, which could be recorded in court minutes.

It's not uncommon to find membership records for several generations of the same family in one guild; however, people who joined through patrimony did not necessarily work in the trade connected to their guild. For instance, a surgeon by the name of Cumberbatch was welcomed into the Company of Spectacle Makers, which is most likely a clue as to his direct ancestor's occupation.

The City of London was home to an endless list of guilds, some incorporated by royal charter which became known as livery companies and developed distinctive uniforms. Records from the 16th century onwards of members of the Clothworkers' Company, the Drapers' Company, the Goldsmiths' Company, the Mercers' Company and other companies in London can be searched online at www.londonroll.org.

Books about the history of your ancestor's company will reveal more about the unique way in which it operated and the grievances of its members. Some older publications can be found at the British Library, such as Charles H Ashdown's 1919 *History of the Worshipful Company of Glaziers of the City of London*.

Most guild members became freemen of the city in which they worked, allowing them to trade freely and enjoy certain privileges. TheGenealogist.co.uk has lists of freemen in Bedford, Canterbury, Chester, Leicester, Norwich, Newcastle and York. Again these records can provide links to several generations of the same family, since the freedom of a city could be passed on to children. In the Register of Freemen of Leicester we find John Agar, a painter, who was the first freeborn son of John Pharez Agar, a tailor, who in turn was the fourth son of Charles Agar.

People could earn the freedom of the city and (until 1832) the right to vote in parliamentary elections by completing an apprenticeship with a freeman. The names of people who were bound to the freemen of Hull can be searched on Hull History Centre's website at www.hullhistorycentre.org.uk/discover/hull_history_centre/our_collections /source_guides/apprenticeship_records.aspx. In admission records for freemen of the City of London held by the London Metropolitan Archives we find traders originating from as far afield as Canterbury and

Cumberland. A freeman's certificate was essentially his licence to trade in the city, and those caught trading without a certificate could face fines. Detailed guidance to locating records for freemen of the City of London is online at **www.cityoflondon.gov.uk/things-to-do/london-metropolitan-archives/visitor-information/Documents/14-city-freedom-archives.pdf**.

A LICENCE TO TRADE

Itinerant traders who were not freemen could seek a licence from a local court to carry on their business. Quarter Sessions Recognizance Rolls include regular lists of licensed 'badgers', also known as peddlars, hawkers or higglers who wore badges as proof of their licence. The same court could indict people for trading without a licence. The Calendars of Worcestershire Quarter Sessions on **TheGenealogist.co.uk** record that William Buttell, William Daye, Clement George, Thomas George and William George, all of Yore Pidell, were presented to the Grand Jury in 1607 for being "common badgers of corn without licence". Quarter Sessions records are held at county record offices but are rarely indexed by name so published calendars like this are invaluable.

Apprenticeship records

Following the 1563 Statute of Artificers and Apprentices it was illegal to start practising a trade without first completing an apprenticeship, usually lasting seven years. Initially the guilds controlled this system. Boys who trained under the watchful eye of a master craftsman could hope for a decent enough life, and the range of trades that could be learnt through an apprenticeship was vast. Among the records we find successful furniture maker Thomas Chippendale and celebrated artist William Blake alongside ordinary coopers and grocers.

A private legal contract known as an indenture was drawn up, which bound the apprentice to his master for a fixed term and fee. These documents, where they survive, name the master, the apprentice, and sometimes their father as well, as they were usually too young to enter a legal agreement alone and many parents paid for their child's apprenticeship. The Society of Genealogists is the custodian of Crisp's Apprentice's Indentures and the London Apprenticeship Abstracts, containing information about thousands of indentures held in local archives.

In 1710 the government introduced a stamp duty on apprenticeship indentures. Records of this tax up to 1811 (around the time the tax was abolished) are held at The National Archives in series IR 1. The registers can be searched by the names of masters or apprentices on

TheGenealogist.co.uk, and occasionally list girls such as Blanch, daughter of Hugh Davey, who was apprenticed to tailor Matthew Harvey in St Ives, Cornwall in 1744. A wide assortment of traders are represented in these records, from apothecaries, bakers and carpenters to shipwrights, toymakers and woolcombers. Names of apprentices' fathers are usually given up to around 1752.

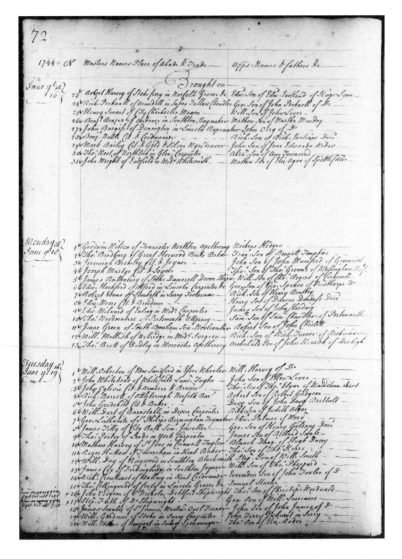

An apprenticeship Stamp Duty register at TheGenealogist.co.uk

Children who found themselves in the workhouse or an industrial school could be enrolled on apprenticeships by the Poor Law authorities or a charitable organisation so that they might learn a trade and be less of a burden upon the public purse. These apprenticeships were not subjected to the stamp duty, but parish records may prove helpful instead. The child could have been sent to live and work with a master well away from their hometown, sometimes in a large mill or factory where they were treated little better than slaves. If this were the case for your ancestor, the Poor Law records for their parish of origin would be the best place to look for any surviving paperwork about their apprenticeship, and should be found in the county archive. Hertfordshire Archives and Local Studies has an Apprentices Index for such cases at **www.hertsdirect.org/services/leisculture/heritage1/hals/ indexes/indexes/apprentice/**. Chester Archives holds an indenture dating from 1741 witnessing that Elizabeth Plefin, whose father had died, was apprenticed to butcher John Holland of Bunbury by the Overseers of the Poor in Baddiley until she attained the age of 21 years. It's doubtful that Elizabeth would have had any say in the matter.

Disputes about apprenticeships could be taken to the Court of Chancery, and summaries of Chancery proceedings from the 14th up to the 18th century are searchable by name on **TheGenealogist.co.uk**. In 1403 Henry Brecknall accused William Wylls of enticing away his apprentice and wrongfully occupying his property in Harberton, Devon (see bpicture below), but Chancery proceedings more typically concerned debts owed to masters for the upkeep of their apprentice, since food and lodging were all part of the deal.

From 1814 it was no longer compulsory to undertake an apprenticeship by indenture in order to legally practise a trade. Informal apprenticeships had become more common prior to the 19th century, and fathers increasingly taught their sons and nephews without need for an indenture. This may explain why you struggle to find official records of an apprenticeship, even if your ancestor is described as an apprentice on the census.

26-29   Peter BOWDEN and Joan his wife, daughter of Margery Palmer, *v.* John BOROUGH.
Lands in Northam of the grant of William Hyllyngs.   DEVON.

30-32   Elizabeth, daughter of John BOWMAN, *v.* Christopher FLETCHER of Cambridge.
Messuage and land in West Wratting.   CAMBRIDGE.

33-34   Edmund BRADOCK, gentleman, *v.* Henry, son and heir of Henry MALKYN.
Messuage and land at Over Longsdon in Leek late of Francis Bradock, esquire, deceased, grand-
father of complainant.   STAFFORD.

35-38   Henry, son and heir of William BRECKNALL, *v.* William WYLLS.
Wrongful occupation of a messuage and land in Harberton, enticing away complainant's apprentice
and frivolous suit.   DEVON, CORNWALL.

39   Richard BREDENAY (?) *v.* John CHECHESTER, esquire.
Refusal to complete a lease of land in Great Torrington. *Damaged.*   DEVON.

Freemasons

The 19th century witnessed a surge in tradesmen joining the secretive fraternity of Freemasons. The word 'freemasonry' is believed to derive from medieval guilds or fellowships of stonemasons, but over time regional lodges emerged that accepted members from all trades and were overseen by Grand Lodges. In contrast to joining a trade guild and becoming a city freeman, there was never a commercial necessity for a tradesperson to become a Freemason, but many chose to do so for the camaraderie, and businessmen could benefit from the support network and the friendships they formed.

The first Grand Lodge opened in London in 1717 but a rival organisation formed in 1751, purporting to be more closely aligned with what it deemed to be 'ancient freemasonry'. They merged in 1813 to form the United Grand Lodge of England, standardising rituals and regalia across the 647 regional lodges then in existence. Hundreds more lodges opened in the wake of both world wars as ex-servicemen wanted to continue the camaraderie they experienced during the war.

Funeral notices and obituaries in newspapers often hint that a person was a member of a freemasonry lodge. **TheGenealogist.co.uk** has a digital edition of the 1913–1914 *Who's Who in Freemasonry*, which can be searched by name or browsed page by page. The entries are illuminating, revealing some lesser-known facts; Thomas Jones, born 1849, was educated at Homerton College, became a wharfinger (wharf keeper) and enjoyed bowling in his spare time. The 1926 *Masonic Who's Who*, also available on TheGenealogist.co.uk, contains biographical information about men from around the world who were associated with the United Grand Lodge of England.

Despite the secretive nature of freemasonry, some membership records do exist. From 1799 until the 1960s, the Seditious Societies Act stipulated that each lodge should submit a list of freemasons' names, their addresses and occupations to the Quarter Sessions. These court records are held in local archives. The Library and Museum of Freemasonry at Freemasons' Hall, 60 Great Queen Street, London WC2B 5AZ also holds annual returns of members of individual lodges, which were sent to the Grand Lodge. These date from 1768 and have been digitised up to 1886 for consultation in the Library and Museum. The minute books of the Grand Lodge provide some earlier 18th-century lists of members.

The Library and Museum offers a family history research service, providing information about former Freemasons for a fee of £30 where

TRADE DIRECTORIES

Directories are especially useful for finding adverts and addresses of people who had their own business. They first appeared in the 17th century and were published annually towards the latter half of the 19th century, usually as county volumes. All County Record Offices have collections of local publications, but TheGenealogist.co.uk has a large digital collection of directories for all over the country, from Bedfordshire to Yorkshire. You can establish a rough timeline for how long the business traded by tracing your ancestor's name through successive volumes. This may also reveal when they moved premises. Many directories contain indexes to the names of advertisers. Adverts provide a unique insight into the goods your ancestor actually produced. An advert in the 1888 Birmingham Directory reveals that cook and confectioner C. Benson sold bridal cakes, wedding breakfasts, jellies, soups, catered for dinners and balls, and ran a 'celebrated a-la-mode beef and sausage establishment.'

52   BIRMINGHAM ADVERTISEMENTS.   [1868.

HENRY ALLEN,

SUCCESSOR TO G. ALLEN,

Rifle, Gun, and Pistol Maker,

AND MANUFACTURER OF THE

IMPROVED DOUBLE & SINGLE BREECH-LOADERS,

15, WEAMAN ROW & 20, RUSSELL STREET, BIRMINGHAM.

JAMES KINGDOM AVIS,

Burnished & Dead Gold, Metal & Colour

TRANSFER PRINTER AND LITHOGRAPHER,

Coventry Road, Small Heath,

BIRMINGHAM.

HENRY BELL,

(ESTABLISHED 1861.)

SCREW RIVET WORKS,

 397, New John St. West, Birmingham,

MANUFACTURER OF

BRASS, COPPER, ZINC & IRON SCREW RIVETS,

Cut Tacks, Tingles, Bills, Nugget Nails,

AND ALL OTHER KINDS OF NAILS, FOR BOOTS;

Escutcheon, Gimp, Pannel, and other kinds of Pins:

SOLE MANUFACTURER OF THE PATENT FANCY BRASS SHOE HEEL TIPS.

C. BENSON,

(ESTABLISHED 1769.)

COOK, CONFECTIONER, &c,

98, BULL STREET, AND UNION PASSAGE, BIRMINGHAM.

Bride Cakes, &c., Jellies, Soups, &c.,

WEDDING BREAKFASTS, DINNERS & BALLS FURNISHED.

THE CELEBRATED A-LA-MODE BEEF AND SAUSAGE ESTABLISHMENT.

EXTENSIVE DINING ROOMS.

Every article in season provided on moderate terms.

N.B.—LUNCHEON BAR, UNION PASSAGE. HOT AND COLD LUNCHEONS.

the lodge name or number are not known, or for free where this information is provided. Apply online at **www.freemasonry. london.museum/family-history/search-request-form/**. The Membership Register should reveal the name of the lodge to which your relative belonged, the date they joined, their address and occupation. You can then research the history of that lodge for further information. The Library and Museum holds many useful sources, including lodge histories, 19th- and 20th-century masonic magazines, and some photographs of past members such as John Henry Clarke, a jeweller turned photographer and the son of a fancy goods merchant, about whom there is much biographical information in the online catalogue. The Library and Museum catalogue can be searched at **www.freemasonry.london.museum**, and staff are able to advise whether a surviving lodge is likely to hold further records. Pat Lewis's book *My Ancestor was a Freemason* (2012) provides an in-depth guide to this subject, and there is an online family history information sheet with additional tips at **freemasonry.london.museum/os/wp-content/ uploads/2010/11/About-Freemasonry-and-Family-History.pdf**.

International trading links

The Company of Merchant Adventurers of London had connections with several enterprises that explored trade overseas from the 16th century. One of these was the East India Company (EIC), granted a Royal Charter in 1600 awarding its London merchants a monopoly on trade with the East Indies. For over 250 years the EIC thrived on purchasing spices, tea, fabrics and, more controversially, opium from India for resale around the world. Its capitalist grip on the country was loosened following the Indian Rebellion of 1857, after which the British Crown assumed control of civil affairs and established a government under the guise of the British Raj.

Commercial links with India presented great opportunities for British merchants and tradespeople who travelled there in their thousands for business purposes. **TheGenealogist.co.uk** has registers and directories for people living and trading in India in 1805, 1820 and 1834, including lists of the East India Company's employees and other Europeans not employed by the EIC. These can be searched from **www.thegenealogist.co.uk/book/volume.php?rec_type=India** and include the names and places of abode of many shopkeepers, as well as farriers, watchmakers, carpenters, butchers and 'free merchants' who tried their luck in the East.

The East India Company archives are now held in the India Office collection in the Asian and African Studies Reading Room at the British Library. They are searchable using the British Library's Archives and Manuscripts catalogue at **www.bl.uk**, with a separate family history database available at **http://indiafamily.bl.uk/ui/home.aspx** drawing on biographical sources for people such as Thomas Abraham, a senior merchant in the East India Company's Bengal Civil Service who drowned in 1818. The Library has a useful guide for researching the lives of merchants and other European migrants in India at **www.bl.uk/ reshelp/findhelpregion/asia/india/indiaofficerecordsfamilyhistory/ occupations/otheroccupations/otheroccupations.html**.

Plenty of skilled tradespeople also came to Britain from abroad, whether for economical or political reasons. Thousands of Protestant silk weavers (Huguenots) forced to flee Catholic France settled around Spitalfields, Norwich, Canterbury and Southampton in the 17th century. Jewish tailors arrived in waves from Eastern Europe throughout the 19th century. Specialist builders and craftspeople came from all over the Continent to share their skills with the native workforce. A great deal of information about the employment history of migrant workers can be gleaned from naturalisation papers if they chose to settle here permanently and applied for similar rights to British citizens.

Lewin Frankenburg's application papers recorded that he was a Russian fancy goods merchant and wholesale dealer in hairdressers' implements who undertook his apprenticeship with a barber in Warsaw from the age of 12 to 18. Lewin arrived in the East End of London in 1906 and three years later purchased a hairdressing establishment at 15 Stoney Lane, which he later converted into a wholesale business. By 1923 his turnover was a staggering £60,000 and he employed nine assistants. These naturalisation papers are held among Home Office documents at The National Archives and detailed guidance about finding original files from various periods is online at **www.nationalarchives.gov.uk/help-with-your-research/research-guides/naturalisation-british-citizenship/**. **TheGenealogist.co.uk** has a database of over 400,000 of these records, dating from 1609 up to 1960, which also include applications for denization, a more affordable option that did not offer as many rights as naturalisation. Find out more at **www.thegenealogist.co.uk/international/naturalisation-denization/**.

Michael Marks, founder of the well-known retail chain Marks & Spencer, features in TheGenealogist.co.uk database of naturalisations.

The Jewish immigrant opened a Penny Bazaar in Leeds in 1884 and 10 years later partnered with Tom Spencer. By 1897 the pair had opened 37 branches and over a century later the firm maintains an impressive archive in the Michael Marks building at the University of Leeds. The Marks & Spencer Company Archive contains over 70,000 items, including employee magazines, photographs, letters and reports, and has a dedicated website at **https://marksintime.marksandspencer.com/the-collection**. The archive catalogue can be searched by keyword or browsed by theme, and the section about employees includes digital copies of photograph albums showing, among other things, the Mile End store's Christmas party in 1955.

Sainsbury's, an even older retail establishment founded in 1869, has an archive held at the Museum of London Docklands. Digital copies of Sainsbury's in-house magazine *JS Journal* published from 1946 can be found online at **http://archive.museumoflondon.org.uk/SainsburyArchive/** and a catalogue of over 16,000 items including staff records and photographs can be searched at **http://catalogue.sainsburyarchive.org.uk/calmview/**. The Archon directory at **http://discovery.nationalarchives.gov.uk/find-an-archive** is useful for establishing whether a firm has its own archive – a search for Boots the chemist reveals it has a records centre in Nottingham holding staff records, photographs and corporate ledgers.

Commercial property

Craftspeople could protect the copyright of their designs for a wide range of commercial products from 1839. The National Archives holds Design Registers for around three million designs registered between 1839 and 1991, including ceramics, metal and woodwork, textiles and wallpaper. The registers recorded the design number, date of registration, name and address of the copyright holder, and sometimes a description of the object. Corresponding volumes of 'representations' were also compiled containing a drawing or photograph of the design, or a sample swatch for paper and fabric designs.

Some of the best surviving examples can be seen online at **https://design.nationalarchives.gov.uk**. Proprietors' names are listed at **www.nationalarchives.gov.uk/designregisters/proprietor.asp** where there are high-resolution images of designs such as an earring registered by Charles Koenig in the mid-19th century, and an ornamental box for playing cards registered by Benjamin Milne of 134 Fleet Street. This online collection represents just a small fragment of the full archive of registered designs, however. The registers up to 1883 can be searched by name using The National Archives' Discovery catalogue and a detailed guide to using this record set is online at **www.nationalarchives.gov.uk/help-with-your-research/research-guides/registered-designs-1839-1991/**.

Many merchants and successful tradespeople left wills mentioning the property they had acquired (see Chapter 5). Probate inventories where they survive in local archives can make for interesting reading, describing the premises and tools of the deceased person's trade and the material possessions they had accumulated. If your ancestor owned or rented premises in England or Wales at the beginning of Queen Victoria's reign then the location of these buildings might be found using the tithe apportionments and maps on **TheGenealogist.co.uk**, which are described in Chapter 1. Deeds or leases may also survive in the county archive, and if your ancestor traded from a shop in a town then J West's *Town Records* (1983) offers some helpful tips for sourcing further documentation, containing a gazetteer of boroughs in England and Wales and the records that survive locally. Twentieth-century telephone directories on TheGenealogist.co.uk include business addresses and telephone numbers, such as F A Abbey's tearooms in Bracken cott Peaslake, Surrey, and builder and contractor H Adams of 22 Lorraine Gardens in Ashtead, who were both in business in 1936.

Distinctive historic buildings associated with trades that have gradually petered out are still scattered across the landscape, remnants of a once thriving rural economy. Many corn exchanges where corn was traded have been converted for some other public use and are accessible today. The magnificent Old Market Hall in Shrewsbury reflects the town's growing prosperity in the late 16th century, and the upper rooms where local drapers and wool merchants displayed their wares have been converted into a film centre and café bar. In picturesque Branscombe, in East Devon, the National Trust looks after the old thatched blacksmith's forge where ironmongery hand-crafted by the resident blacksmith can still be purchased.

The Mills Archive Trust cares for records about historic windmills and watermills, including photographs, pictures, deeds and architectural drawings, and also has a large collection of correspondence, ledgers and wage books kept by traditional millers. Its library houses an extensive collection of mill-related journals and trade literature, and the archive and library collections can be explored at **https://millsarchive.org**.

The dawn of the Industrial Age hit rural traders and craftsmen hard.

Unable to compete with the prices of mass-produced goods, many skilled workers and their children were forced to find work in gigantic factories and modern mills. Between 1811 and 1813 groups of artisan textile workers in Nottinghamshire, Yorkshire and Lancashire organised midnight raids, systematically breaking into premises to destroy thousands of new weaving frames and machinery that threatened their livelihoods. They issued written proclamations in the name of a fictitious character called 'General Ludd', and became known as the Luddites. The problem was taken so seriously by the government of the day that the Frame Breaking Act of 1812 introduced the death penalty for such crimes. Remarkably few Luddites were ever caught but local newspapers are good sources for finding convictions and the history of this close-knit community can be researched at **www.luddites200.org.uk**. Their revolt was eventually crushed, and by the time Queen Victoria came to the throne the dark satanic mills conjured up in William Blake's famous poem were a permanent feature in the landscape. Nothing stood in the way of economic progress.

A weaver at work

Chapter Three: Industry

Technological advances in the 18th and 19th centuries transformed cottage industries, generating factories on an unimaginable scale. Sir Richard Arkwright created a blueprint for massive mills powered by watercourses out in the countryside, where additional housing needed to be built to accommodate the growing industrial workforce. Villages were turned into towns and, when sufficient coal was produced to replace water power, more factories sprang up in urban centres such as Manchester, Birmingham and Sheffield, transforming them into cities.

Factories, foundries, mills and mines were privately-run enterprises, often owned by powerful capitalists and wealthy landed families, until the mid-20th century when some industries were nationalised. Therefore, any surviving records prior to nationalisation will most likely be found in local archives among company or family estate papers. The volume of Records of British Business And Industry 1760–1914 dealing with metal processing and engineering contains an index by town and county for steel works, iron foundries and engineering companies. The National Archives' Discovery catalogue (**http://discovery.nationalarchives.gov.uk**) is also useful for identifying the whereabouts of records created by companies, families and individuals, like the factory registers and staff records created by ironfounder Daniel Clarke, now held in Cumbria Archive Centre. There is a far greater chance of finding records for the owners and managers of these businesses than the ordinary workers, however.

Their names occasionally appear in the reports of Royal Commissions and Parliamentary Committees set up to enquire into working conditions; for example, in the 1830s a Select Committee interviewed 89 children employed in textile factories and their testimony was published in MP Michael Sadler's report. Matthew Crabtree's distressing evidence can be read at **www.victorianweb.org/history/workers1.html**. The blanket manufacturer recalled having to work 16-hour shifts with just an hour's break from the age of eight and being beaten regularly for drowsiness. His testimony and the recollections of other workers ultimately resulted in the Factory Act enforcing maximum working hours for children.

Productivity soared nevertheless and Britain prospered from the misery inflicted on its workers. Besides the super-rich industrialists there were also thousands of Victorian entrepreneurs who set up smaller workshops and factories in Britain's ever-expanding towns and cities. Grace's Guide to British Industrial History (**www.gracesguide.co.uk**) is an invaluable online resource, containing information about a diverse range of industrial enterprises extracted from *The Engineering Times* and other journals, and publications of the Institute of Mechanical Engineers and the Institute of Civil Engineers. Many of these journals have been digitised and can be viewed for free online. A search for Birmingham manufacturers Edmund Eaborn and Matthew Robinson's firm locates an advert for their steam-powered malt-crushing machine in the *Staffordshire Sentinel* newspaper, as well as an illustration of their sugar-crushing machine published in *The Engineer* in 1857.

Trade directories, mentioned in the last chapter, are also handy for finding adverts and listings for manufacturers. They are arranged by county, but annual volumes can be searched by name using **TheGenealogist.co.uk**. Whellan's 1853 Directory of Manchester includes information about outlying towns and villages, and contains a detailed description of New Mills, a township formed in the mid 18th century that relied enormously on the cotton trade. Iron founders, lime burners, tanners and curriers, paper manufacturers and a cotton waste dealer are listed in the directory for New Mills alongside the local clog maker, time keeper and town crier.

Some larger employers built cheap workers' housing, so finding ancestors on census returns living within a factory complex or in mining cottages can provide a clue as to where they worked and for whom. Old maps may be useful for establishing which collieries or factories operated in your ancestors' neighbourhood if you aren't sure exactly where they were employed; however, in the late 19th century an overwhelming number of available options could make it difficult to start looking for further employment records. The online Coal Mining History Resource Centre at **www.cmhrc.co.uk** has maps for locating collieries around the country plus a wealth of literature on the subject, including an article describing a day in a miner's life published in the *Picture Post* in 1939. Researching the development of industries in your ancestors' locale gives a flavour of what their working life would have been like even if you can't establish exactly where they clocked on each day.

The best way to get to grips with their daily routine is to visit one of the many museums dedicated to preserving the history of Britain's industrial past. The Black Country Living Museum (**www.bclm.co.uk**) is set in 26 acres of former industrial land in the West Midlands – arguably the most intensely industrialised region of the country. People researching roots in this area would be well advised to pick up Michael Pearson's book *Tracing Your Black Country Ancestors* (2012). At the museum, trams transport visitors around a canalside village, complete with Victorian shops. Community buildings that were a common feature of industrial towns have been reconstructed at the heart of the village, including public baths, the Workers' Institute and chapel, alongside workshops, a forge, rolling mill and an underground mine.

In a similar vein, Beamish Living Museum in County Durham (www.beamish.org.uk) explores the impact that industrialisation had on ordinary families from the 1820s through to the 1940s. A circular tramway at the open-air museum connects its Georgian landscape to a 1900s pit village and town where there is a reconstructed colliery, as well as a 1940s farm. The museum has also compiled a 'People's Collection' of photos, audio recordings, objects and catalogued collections of records from industries across the North that can be searched by keyword at http://collections.beamish.org.uk.

WHO'S WHO IN YORKSHIRE

TheGenealogist.co.uk has a digital copy of *Who's Who in Yorkshire* dating from 1912, containing short biographies for industrialists and successful businesspeople who lived and worked in the county. Joseph Archer, born in 1842 in Derbyshire, worked for many years in Sheffield and received a mention for his career as a mineral agent and mining engineer. Archer's entry provides plenty of genealogical information about his parents, grandparents, wife and children, and also reveals details about his education and the various companies he worked for before he became a Director at Skinner & Holford Ltd., which owned Waleswood Collieries near Sheffield.

Miners

Coal powered the Industrial Revolution during Queen Victoria's reign. In 1841 over 190,000 men, women and children were employed in mines, more than half of them in coal mines. By 1920 the number of employees in the coal mining industry had risen to 1,248,000. A Royal Commission reported on the shocking working conditions of miners throughout the country in 1842, confirming rumours that young women and children worked almost naked, suffering unbearable temperatures in cramped tunnels below ground. The Commission's illustrated reports containing evidence given by miners can be read at **www.cmhrc.co.uk/site/ literature/royalcommissionreports/**. Though incremental changes were made to legislation throughout the 19th century to protect the very young and limit working hours, in reality conditions had improved little by the 20th century. Collier George Kemp, born 1920, recalled working a seam on his knees in a space just 2 feet 8 inches high, and when the call of nature needed to be answered, "well you just had to manage where you were working".

If your mining ancestor was employed after 1947, when the coal industry was nationalised, you can apply for a copy of their National Coal Board employment record from Iron Mountain Records Management, PO Box 3238, Stafford, ST16 9LS (tel 0844 2641 486). This is a free service if you know the miner's full name, date of birth and preferably their National Insurance number and the last colliery they worked at. The records include a medical record card and notices of accidents or dangerous incidents.

The libraries of the National Coal Mining Museum for England in Wakefield (**www.ncm.org.uk**) and the North of England Institute of Mining and Mechanical Engineers in Newcastle upon Tyne (**www.mininginstitute.org.uk/collections**) house books, journals, photos and ephemera useful for researching collieries and the history of the industry in particular regions. The Mining History Network at **http://projects.exeter.ac.uk/mhn/welcome.html** also points to a large number of useful secondary sources and societies for researching mining communities.

Digital copies of *Coal* magazine published from 1947 to 1960 can be read on the NCM Museum for England website at **www.ncmonline.org.uk/coal_magazine**. In a regular feature, 'Pit Profile', the magazine commissioned an artist to draw portraits of distinguished members of local mining communities, which were published along with a short biography. Griffith Thomas, mechanic at Seven Sisters Colliery in Glamorgan for over 40 years, was pictured in the first issue. Griffith had "proved his faith in the future of British mining by the gift of six virile sons into its ranks".

You can descend underground in a pit cage with a former miner and experience life at the coalface at the Big Pit National Coal Museum for Wales in Blaenafon (**www.museumwales.ac.uk/bigpit/**). The NCM

Museum for England also conducts tours 140 metres underground. Durham Mining Museum website **www.dmm.org.uk** contains an enormous range of useful resources for researching miners in the North of England, including a Memorial Roll for those who perished in mining disasters, lists of workers for some collieries, and a huge directory of mining companies revealing the dates they were active and the names of owners and managers. It also contains information about a peculiar system of serfdom that persisted in the northeast of England until 1872, whereby miners were bonded to a master on a fixed quarterly or annual contract without the promise of work.

The North of England Lead Mining Museum at Killhope in County Durham (**www.killhope.org.uk**) is the best preserved lead mine in Britain. Visitors are taken on underground guided tours of the site, known as Park Level Mine and Park Level Mill, which opened in 1853 at the centre of the North Pennines, an area once strewn with lead mines. Further south, the Peak District Lead Mining Museum in Matlock holds the reference library for the Peak District Mines Historical Society and recommends a trip to Derbyshire Record Office for anyone researching mining ancestors from that region, while the Chatsworth Estate archive at Chatsworth House also holds some material about mines owned by the Dukes of Devonshire. Cleveland Ironstone Mining Museum offers a family history look-up service to establish whether an ancestor's name appears in their collection of pay books, accident books, company letters and union minutes. Just fill in the form at **http://ironstonemuseum.co.uk/family-history/**.

While the north of England and Wales are associated with coal, lead and ironstone mines, Cornwall and Devon were exploited for their rich seams of copper and tin. Ten areas in the southwest have now been designated part of the Cornish Mining World Heritage Site (**www.cornish-mining.org.uk**), including King Edward Mine in Troon, the oldest complete Cornish mine. The history of individual mines in Cornwall is summarised online at **www.cornwall-calling.co.uk/mines.htm**, covering clay and slate mines as well as copper and tin. Tin mines are known as stannaries and, as early as the Middle Ages, Stannary Courts were formed to administer justice within tin mining communities. The Stannary Courts and Parliaments were not abolished until 1896 and their records are now held primarily at Cornwall Record Office.

Almost all mining communities were touched by tragedy at some point. There is an alphabetical list of mining disasters at **www.cmhrc.pwp.blueyonder.co.uk/lodisalp.htm** and footage capturing the aftermath of pit accidents in the 20th century can even be watched for free on the British Pathé website. A film from 1919 at **www.britishpathe.com/video/cornish-tin-mine-disaster/query/mining** shows miners and a broken shaft that fell at Levant Tin Mine in St Just, Cornwall, resulting in a heavy death toll.

Mining in the southwest declined during the mid 19th century when tin rushes overseas created competition in the home market. Migration from tin mining areas was therefore high as workers sought employment elsewhere. It was a different story in the southeast of England, however, after coal was discovered near Dover in 1890. Dover Museum's Coalfields Heritage Initiative Kent (CHIK) project at **www.dovermuseum.co.uk/Exhibitions/Coal-Mining-in-Kent/Coal-Mining-in-Kent.aspx** charts the history of the coalfields there, which attracted miners to settle in Kent from across the North and the Midlands. For an in-depth guide to researching miners from all over the country, turn to David Tonks's book *My Ancestor was a Coalminer* (2003).

Factories, foundries and mills

The endless toil of workers in towns across the North kept Britain's industrial heart beating. Foundries spawned around mining areas, where extracted metals were moulded into everything from spoons to steam engine components. Machinery that manufactured a bewildering plethora of products pumped on through the night, minded by children under the age of nine until the 1833 Factory Act raised the minimum age of child labour. Appallingly, though, the minimum age was only raised from 10 to 11 as late as 1891.

Cotton production was Britain's most valuable industry, employing thousands of hands at mechanised looms in Lancashire, Cheshire, Derbyshire and Yorkshire. Factory workers in Bradford and Halifax focused on wool and worsted production. Giant flourmills started to replace traditional windmills from the 1880s, opening close to major ports including Liverpool, Hull and London where wheat could be imported cheaply. The census returns taken between 1841 and 1911 reveal whole families left the countryside behind to become townies, enticed by the prospect of regular employment and higher wages.

Some orphaned and poor children were sent away to work in factories under the Poor Law apprenticeship schemes mentioned in the previous chapter. You may also find evidence in Poor Law records of ancestors experiencing the effects of the Lancashire Cotton Famine in 1861–1865. The famine was a result of blockades on American ports during the Civil War, which stopped cotton from reaching Lancashire mills and led to widespread unemployment. Spinning the Web at **www.spinningtheweb.org.uk** has garnered 20,000 documents, photos, articles and reports from libraries, museums and archives across Lancashire to tell the story of the cotton industry from the perspective of mill owners, managers and workers. The Cotton Town website at **www.cottontown.org** does a similar job, focusing on the Blackburn with Darwen area, and contains transcripts from old newspaper interviews with former residents such as Charles Holt Stirrup who in 1933 recalled stones being thrown through windows during the cotton riots of the 1880s.

Records were created as a result of changes to the law aimed at improving industrial workers' conditions during the Victorian period. The Education Act of 1870 stipulated that all children under the age of 10 should be in full-time education, and combined with the Factory Acts it became illegal to employ them. School Leaving Certificates were issued to prove that a child had completed his or her education and was free to be employed, and these sometimes survive within company records. Inspectors also paid visits to factories to ensure the various Factory Acts from 1833 onwards were being abided. Inspectors' reports might therefore be found in local record offices, and Factory Inspectors' Registers kept by businesses may survive, which can include information about employees. Prosecutions against industrialists and managers who failed to uphold the law were reported in the local press. The Workmen's Compensation Act introduced in 1897 and extended in 1906 allowed people to claim compensation for injury at work and the company had to keep official record books listing claims. Since most of these documents will be found within company records, it's usually necessary to know which company your ancestor worked for.

In a beautiful building designed by Basil Champney, John Rylands University Library (**www.library.manchester.ac.uk/rylands/**), part of the University of Manchester, holds papers deposited by local landed families, business associations, trade unions and social organisations, such as the archive of the Amalgamated Association of Operative Cotton Spinners and Twiners, which includes benefit registers, wage lists and minute books dating from 1878 to 1977. The John Rylands University Library archive collections can be searched at **http://archives.li.man.ac.uk/ead/**.

Journals are likely to be useful for researching the manufacturing elite. Manchester County Record Office holds copies of some locally published ones, including the *Textile Manufacturer* (1897–1914), *Textile Recorder* (1884–1967) and *Textile Weekly* (1928–1967). The British Library has an enormous collection of trade journals published nationally, like *Wool Record and Cotton Factory Times*, which can be found using the advanced function on the 'Explore the British Library' Catalogue.

There are plenty of museums where you can learn about the rise of your ancestor's industry. The Derwent Valley Mills in Derbyshire, where Arkwright and other wealthy businessmen revolutionised the textile industry, have been recognised as the birthplace of the factory system, for which they have been awarded UNESCO World Heritage status (**www.derwentvalleymills.org**). Bradford Industrial Museum, housed in a former worsted-spinning mill built in 1875, has permanent displays of textile machinery alongside temporary exhibitions. Visitors to the West Yorkshire site can tour the mill workers' cottages and mill manager's house to see how the company's employees lived (**www.bradfordmuseums.org**).

Sheffield in South Yorkshire was famed for its steel and cutlery production until many foundries closed in the 1970s and 1980s. Sheffield Industrial Museums Trust now runs Kelham Island Museum demonstrating what it was like to live and work in the steelmaking capital of the world. The museum also houses the Trust's archive collection of manufacturing company records, which can be searched at **http://discovery.nationalarchives.gov.uk** using the advanced function. The Abbeydale Industrial Hamlet also run by the trust preserves an 18th-century scythe and steelworks, and at Shepherd Wheel you can see knife-grinding machinery in action. The indexes at **www.sheffieldrecordsonline.org.uk/index_cutlers.html** reveal master cutlers and apprentices who belonged to the Company of Cutlers in Hallamshire up to 1925 and 1858 respectively.

If your ancestor worked for a major manufacturer that is still in business then the company may have its own archives. Cadbury's first chocolate factory opened in Birmingham in 1847 and its pioneering Bournville factory and surrounding workers' village opened in 1879. By 1930 the firm was the 24th largest manufacturer in Britain. Records of Bournville tenants are held among the Bournville Village Trust Archive at Birmingham Archives and Heritage Centre.

The Institute of Mechanical Engineers in London maintains a library and archive of memberships records, personal papers and company records for firms that were involved in engineering machinery, engine builders, automobile production and railway engineering. Find out more at **www.imeche.org/knowledge/library/archive**.

ILLUSTRATED LONDON NEWS

Phenomenal feats of industry were reported in the *Illustrated London News*, which brimmed with bulletins about the Great Exhibition at Hyde Park, organised by Prince Albert in 1851 to showcase Britain's manufacturing might. The *Illustrated London News* can be searched by keyword on **TheGenealogist.co.uk** and includes published lists of medals awarded at the exhibition to individuals and firms like Samuel Cocker & Son for the quality of their steel.

Transport workers

Materials were primarily transported on horse-drawn barges via a vast network of man-made canals when the Industrial Revolution started to gather momentum in the 18th century. These inland waterways were built by private investment companies from the late 17th century, and by the 1830s over 4000 miles of canals had been dug by rival firms that made huge profits carrying coal, timber, building materials and all manner of heavy goods.

Sue Wilkes' book *Tracing Your Canal Ancestors* (2011) covers the intricacies of researching canal boatmen who lived with their families on the waterways, and explains why they can be difficult to trace. Perhaps census enumerators gave up easily when faced with the prospect of a muddy walk along the towpath to ask questions of rough and ready bargemen? Not all were unforthcoming though. The 1901 census for Anderton in Northwich on **TheGenealogist.co.uk** (below) recorded whole families aboard canal boats called 'The Lark', 'Caballros', 'Fred', 'Civic',

'City of Rome' and so on. This information is invaluable for searching for sanitary inspection registers of canal boats at local archives. Officially known as Health (Canal Boat) Registers, they were compiled from 1877 by local authorities and the ones that survive may give the name of the company that the boat master worked for. Gauging records created for each boat also provide this information, and indicate the type of freight that was carried.

The Waterways Archive at the National Waterways Museum at Ellesmere Port is the national repository for the canal network. It holds the archives of British Waterways and some early canal companies. The online catalogue can be searched at **http://collections.canalrivertrust.org.uk** and the archive also offers a research service (see **https://canalrivertrust.org.uk/national-waterways-museum/the-museum-collections/the-waterways-archive**). The museum has partnered with several other archives to create the Virtual Waterways Archive Catalogue at **www.virtualwaterways.co.uk**, with over 40,000 digital records including personal work diaries, company accounts, plans and drawings.

The Canal and River Trust suggests places to visit all over the country at **https://canalrivertrust.org.uk**. A website dedicated to the history of Gloucester Docks and the Sharpness Canal has information about finding canal boat registers, port books, pilotage records, crew lists and ships' registers at Gloucestershire Archives at **www.gloucesterdocks.me.uk/people/familyresearch.htm**, while The Weavers' Triangle Visitor Centre at Burnley Wharf by the Leeds and Liverpool Canal explores how the canal served the local textile industry (**www.weaverstriangle.co.uk**).

The Liverpool and Manchester Railway was the first regular railway to open in 1830, and by the mid 19th century the canal companies were feeling the pinch of competition as more privately-run railway companies extended tracks across the country. Some railway companies bought out canal companies so they could operate their routes, and over time canals were filled in as they became less profitable and replaced by new railway lines or by roads. When the railways were nationalised in 1947, the Government inherited the records of private railway companies and the old canal companies they had acquired. Therefore The National Archives has a large collection of papers for railway and canal companies dating from the 19th century and earlier, including staff registers, salary registers and other personnel records. These are held in the RAIL series, though record survival is patchy and mostly covers larger firms like the Great Western Railway Company (GWR).

To find a staff record you usually need to know which railway company your ancestor worked for (this is sometimes noted on census returns in abbreviated form), and their job title to establish which department they belonged to. Smaller railway companies were often bought out or merged with larger conglomerates, and so the records of both companies may need to be checked. There is detailed guidance to accessing the RAIL series at **www.nationalarchives.gov.uk/help-with-your-research/research-guides/railway-workers/**.

To speed up the process, **TheGenealogist.co.uk** has indexes to some of The National Archives' railway employees' records, taken from RAIL 134/40 listing GWR staff in 1889, part of series RAIL 264 comprising further GWR staff records, part of RAIL 236 covering records of the Great Northern Railway (GNR), and also digital copies of staff magazines that contain information about promotions, staff movements, retirements, pensions and obituaries. For example, the *Great Western Railway Magazine* of 1927 recorded the movement of gang labourer F G Giddins from the Signal Department at Machynlleth to Shrewsbury, and the *British Railways Magazine* for the western region reported the death of Mr F S Angell in 1950 at the age of 63, who was a former yard master at Bristol's East Depot and had retired the previous year.

The National Railway Museum archive in York holds a large collection of staff magazines, as well as engine drivers' diaries and logbooks, Board of Trade and Ministry of Transport railway accident reports from 1855, photographs, books and unique papers deposited by individuals and families connected to the railways (see **www.nrm.org.uk/Research AndArchive.aspx**). Records of British Rail employees after 1947 were dispersed to County Record Offices for each of the British Rail regions. Turn to Frank Hardy's book *My Ancestor was a Railway Worker* (2009) and David T Hawkins's *Railway Ancestors: A Guide to the Staff Records of the Railway Companies of England and Wales 1822–1947* (2008) for further assistance.

Inland waterways and railways connected manufacturers to ports where they could collect shipments of raw materials and export British goods across the globe. The PortCities website celebrating the history of Bristol, Southampton and London at **www.portcities.org.uk** is no longer updated but still a fantastic source of digital photographs and helpful articles about shipping communities.

Lightermen who dealt with cargo transported on Thames barges, and watermen who ferried passengers, had to belong to the Company of

Watermen and Lightermen. The Company's records prior to c1890 are held at the London Metropolitan Archives (there's an in-depth guide at **www.cityoflondon.gov.uk/things-to-do/london-metropolitan-archives/visitor-information/Documents/18-records-of-the-company-of-watermen-and-lightermen.pdf**), and after that date Watermen's Hall offers a research service (see **www.watermenshall.org/ancestors.html**). James W Legon's book *My Ancestors were Thames Watermen* (2008) may also come in handy for researching this fascinating community.

The lightermen assisted stevedores with loading and unloading cargo between barges and ships, while dockers worked mostly on the quayside. The study centre at the Museum of London Docklands holds records for some men employed permanently on Port of London Authority docks after 1909 (**www.museumoflondon.org.uk/collections-research/research/**). Unfortunately most dockers were employed by private dock companies on a casual basis and paid by the day or just a half-day to unload cargo as it came in. The temporary nature of such work means that there are often no surviving records. The Museum does however hold some records for staff employed permanently by private companies created from the 19th century, such as the London & St Katharine's Dock Company.

The Maritime Archives and Library at Merseyside Maritime Museum houses records of the Mersey Docks and Harbour Board where evidence has been found of women employed as lighthouse keepers. It also holds papers deposited by local shipping lines and merchants. There are information sheets at **www.liverpoolmuseums.org.uk/maritime/archive/** for researching a wide range of subjects including the Liverpool Pilot Service, covering pilots' character books for men employed to assist ships navigating the Port of Liverpool, registers of Masters and Mates holding Pilot's Certificates, and registers of unemployed people on the Pilot Boat Service. Local archive services are often the best place to look for records relating to companies and workers connected to ports. Tyne and Wear Archives has a rich collection of shipbuilders' archives and records for local ship owners as well as the Sunderland Pilotage Authority.

The National Maritime Museum's Caird Library in Greenwich contains a large collection of shipping company archives, Merchant Navy crew lists and Masters' Certificates, which can be searched using the catalogues at **www.rmg.co.uk/researchers/collections**. The National Maritime Museum's research guides for tracing Merchant Navy seamen and officers, shipping company records, ship wrecks and other maritime subjects are particularly thorough, covering not only records held by the library but also The National Archives and overseas repositories (go to www.rmg.co.uk/researchers/library/research-guides). Dr Simon Wills's book *Tracing Your Merchant Navy Ancestors* (2012) describes the expansion of the commercial merchant service and explains how to find records for ships and ancestors who served during times of peace and war, when transporting cargo across the sea became even more perilous.

Labour movements

Given the intensity of industrial work, it is hardly surprising that the 19th century heralded wave after wave of organised labour movements seeking to improve the worker's lot. In the 1830s and 1840s the London Working Men's Association began agitating for political reform to extend the vote to all men, setting out a charter containing their demands. The Chartists, as they became known, petitioned the government in 1838, 1842 and again in 1848, gaining support from industrial workers in the North who went out on general strike. The Chartist Ancestors website www.chartists.net names some of the millions who signed the petitions and were arrested, putting their lives on the line during one of the biggest working class movements since the Peasants' Revolt in the 14th century.

The Chartists were not immediately successful in their aims; however, the movement marked the start of an era that saw small trade organisations reform and radicalise into societies that offered benefits to members and sought to negotiate with employers. Mark Crail's book *Tracing Your Labour Movement Ancestors* (2009) is an invaluable guide for family historians, plotting key events from before the Chartist struggles through to the creation of Victorian socialist societies later in the 19th century, and the establishment of the Labour Party and politically vocal trade unions in the 20th century, while simultaneously explaining the records that they left behind. As Crail points out, more than 5000 trade unions have been active in the UK over the last 200 years, some only short-lived, so it can be a frustrating task trying to find out which ones your ancestor might have belonged to. Interestingly, although the number of trade unions has been steadily falling since 1900, union membership reached an all time high in 1980, peaking at 13 million people compared to just 4 million people belonging to a union in 1900.

The 13-volume *Dictionary of Labour Biography* names some of the more prominent voices in the movement for workers' rights. Establishing exactly what your ancestor's job title was, what materials they worked with, where they were based and when they were employed will help to pinpoint the relevant societies or unions that represented them. The Trade Union Ancestors website set up by Crail at **www.unionancestors.co.uk** has an A–Z list of known trade unions, including small regional organisations like the Macclesfield District Power Loom Overlookers' Association. The six-volume *Historical Directory of Trade Unions*, available in The National Archives' Library, provides information about when each union operated and how large its membership was.

The National Register of Archives and Access to Archives databases have recently been integrated into The National Archives' Discovery catalogue, so searching for an organisation name at **http://discovery.nationalarchives.gov.uk** can reveal where in the country their records are deposited. For example, the records of the National Union of Mineworkers' Northumberland Mechanics Branch are kept at Northumberland Archives and include contribution books, branch correspondence and registers, medical appeal claims and other files. Union archives might also contain admission books, membership lists and cards, minute books and other branch records. The names of union officers and secretaries often appear in meeting minutes, and a record may have been made when union members received payments in times of sickness or old age. The names of members who had died are sometimes listed in the end of year annual report. Union magazines and journals were published in the 20th century to keep members up to date with news, and contain obituaries and articles about special achievements and events.

Besides regional branch material deposited in County Record Offices, there are also several specialist libraries dedicated to labour movement history in Britain, which hold some of the records described above. The Modern Records Centre at the University of Warwick Library has a huge collection of archive material donated by trade unions (searchable at **http://mrc-catalogue.warwick.ac.uk**), including records of the Transport and General Workers' Union, as well as the Trade Union Congress (TUC) official archive of reports, minutes and other papers dating back to 1868. The TUC Library Collections are deposited at the London Metropolitan University, while the TUC History Online website **www.unionhistory.info** includes scanned and searchable copies of TUC annual reports from 1868 to 1968, and photos and lists of Bryant & May's female employees who took to the streets during the Matchworkers' Strike of 1888.

The Working Class Movement Library in Salford holds some of the earliest trade union records, dating back to the 1820s. As well as secondary sources and ephemera there are also union membership records and personal papers of prominent players. There is an introduction to its online catalogue and advice about uncatalogued material at **www.wcml.org.uk/search-the-catalogue/catalogue-introduction/**. The People's History Museum in Manchester (**www.phm.org.uk**) is a good place to go to capture the spirit of the labour movement. The museum is also home to the Labour History Archive and Study Centre, documenting political activism through the ages and containing the archives of the Labour Party from 1900, New Labour and the Communist Party from 1943. Not all of its collections of photographs, newspapers, pamphlets and political papers are catalogued online, but staff will answer enquiries to determine whether they hold material that might interest you.

The Trades Union Congress meeting in Edinburgh, 1897

Was your ancestor in
the legal profession?

Chapter Four: Professionals

The wealth flowing into Britain gradually trickled down to lower levels of society in the 19th century. As Britain's population became better educated and increasingly affluent, business opportunities opened up to a wider number of people. Census enumerators counted growing numbers of domestic servants employed in middle class homes where the head of the household brought in a decent income from a job in the city. Company directors and managers, legal practices and banks employed armies of clerks, agents, secretaries and assistants, and it is to this group of workers that we now turn. We will also look at 'office holders' of government and religious organisations, and at medics and teachers. Some of the sources described in Chapter 2 about craftsmen, tradesmen and merchants will be equally applicable to ancestors considered to be among the 'professional class', since they too could join specialist guilds, become Freemasons and they advertised their services in trade directories. There is also a decent chance of finding material written by this class of competent readers and writers.

The East India Company discussed in Chapter 2 also employed a large number of white collar workers, and the company's archive at the British Library is equally helpful for finding out more about a wide range of employees, from administrators and advocates to civil servants and writers. A list of guides for various occupations can be found at **www.bl.uk/reshelp/findhelpregion/asia/india/indiaofficerecordsfamily history/occupations/occupations.html** and the administrative arrangement of the records is described in detail at **www.bl.uk/reshelp/findhelpregion/asia/india/indiaofficerecords/india officearrangement/indiaofficearrangedrecord.html**.

From 1844 a series of Acts allowed companies to be incorporated through a registration process so that a Royal Charter or statute was no longer necessary. This enabled business to boom, and by 1976 over a million companies had been registered. Again, the National Register of Archives is a good place to start a search for any surviving company papers. Select 'Record creators' at **http://discovery.nationalarchives.gov.uk/advanced-search** and choose 'business' from the list of creators, then enter the name of the company that your ancestor worked for in the keyword box. If this does not yield any results then the Business Archives Council (**www.business archivescouncil.org.uk**), which encourages companies to hold onto their archives, may be able to help you source surviving records for larger organisations. E D Probert's *Company and Business Records for Family Historians* (1994) also offers useful guidance.

Of course it's not always apparent which company an ancestor worked for from the information given on censuses and civil registration certificates alone. Annual directories can again come in handy here. More than 31,000 people are named in the *Directory of Directors* for 1936 available to search on **TheGenealogist.co.uk**, where we learn that Mr G F Abell was the chief general manager of Lloyds Bank on Lombard Street in London, and that Mr Samuel Ackerley of Brett & Co. solicitors in Manchester was also on the local board of the Liverpool and London and Globe Insurance Company. This directory first appeared in 1879, and the British Library holds annual editions up to 2009. The sections below suggest other sources that are searchable by name and which can help you to establish exactly where your ancestors worked or were educated in order to start looking for more archival records.

Education

The Education Acts of 1870 and 1880 were the first pieces of legislation to provide affordable, compulsory schooling for all children up to the age of 10. Previously schools were opened on an ad hoc basis by religious organisations, or were privately funded. Many of the old schools continued to operate after the new School Boards built nondenominational National Schools to ensure that every child could receive an education. Improvements in literacy levels meant that a wider range of employment opportunities were within the reach of youngsters from the lower levels of society. Most people who worked within the professions described in this chapter would have received an education, and there are a number of sources available to research their formative years.

National Schools and some voluntary schools kept registers showing the date each child joined and left the school. Log books kept by the headmaster record special or unusual events and reasons for absences. The local county record office usually holds these (in some cases the school maintains its own historic records), and **TheGenealogist.co.uk** has an extensive collection of printed school registers that can be quickly searched by name (see the box opposite).

Some children stayed on to become 'pupil teachers'. In 1902 Local Education Authorities (LEAs) started to build training colleges. The same year, the Teachers' Registration Council was established to maintain a

SCHOOL REGISTERS

Schools and colleges in Alnwick, Bradfield, Bury St Edmunds, Canterbury, Carlisle, Colchester, Cheltenham, Dover, Durham, Epsom, Harrow, Leeds, Marlborough, Malvern, Rugby, Sedbergh, Shrewsbury, Tiverton, Uppingham and elsewhere are covered in **TheGenealogist.co.uk**'s collection of registers that spans from the 12th century to the mid 20th century. Eton School features alongside alumni lists for Oxford and Cambridge University. The entry for William Wordsworth in Cambridge University's register for St John The Evangelist College warrants a full two pages, while the entry for lawyer James Alexander Wright is almost as detailed, providing summaries of the careers of a long line of legal practitioners from whom he descended.

voluntary register of teachers. The register began properly in 1914 and lasted until 1948. **TheGenealogist.co.uk** holds the *Official List of Registered Teachers* from 1917 published by the Teachers Registration Council. This list gives the registration number of each teacher, the date they registered and the school at which they worked. The Society of Genealogists' Library in London holds the Council's original registers spanning 1914 to 1948, with a sheet for each teacher recording any certificates or degrees they had attained, and details of where they trained as a teacher and the schools where they had taught, sometimes dating back to the 1870s.

The school registers on **TheGenealogist.co.uk** include pages dedicated to headmasters and assistant masters, with short biographies about their earlier careers, the subjects they taught and when they were appointed and departed the school. If your teaching ancestor signed up to fight during World War One then they may feature in the National Union of Teachers War Record 1914–1919, also available to search at the site. In this volume, lists of 'The Gallant Dead' include the name of the school at which the deceased last worked, and there is also a separate list of all members of the National Union of Teachers who joined the Army or Navy, as well as female teachers who acted as nurses. The Roll of Honour and War List, 1914–18, of University College School, Hampstead, again searchable on TheGenealogist.co.uk, contains biographies of members of staff that fell victim to the war. H F E Edwardes, 3rd Master of the 4th Classical Form, is described as "a man not easy at first to get on with on account of his shyness, he was, nevertheless, soon beloved by all". The biography records that Edwardes studied for an MA at Cambridge. Lecturers at Oxford and Cambridge University needed to first be ordained as Anglican clergymen, about whom there is more information overleaf.

Religious vocations

Those with Anglican clergymen in their family tree are particularly lucky because records are plentiful. The parish priest was a community figurehead and photographic portraits often survive within local archive collections. There may also be references to him and his family in local newspapers, or in the *Church Times* published independently since 1863. The Clergy of the Church of England Database at **http://theclergydatabase.org.uk** covers 1540–1835, a period when the Church was the most important employer of educated men. It brings together information found in diocesan registers recording dates of ordination, subscription books, licensing books and liber cleri (or call books). The entry for Jane Austen's father, the Rev George Austen, shows his appointment as the rector of Steventon in 1761, and then as the rector of Deane in 1773. The database also reveals that George Austen studied at St John's College, Oxford, in the 1750s.

The Clergy List, published from 1841 until 1917, and *Crockford's Clerical Directory* published regularly since 1858 can be found at The National Archives and other large repositories, and are worth looking at if an ancestor is described as a clergyman on the census. Crockford's is arranged alphabetically by name, showing where each man was educated, where they were ordained, the parish they were working in at the time of publication, and the dates they were installed in any other parishes previously, so you can track their career. **TheGenealogist.co.uk** has a digital selection of Crockford's and The Clergy List dating from 1852, 1907, 1911 and 1929, as well as the *Index Ecclesiasticus*, containing alphabetical lists of ecclesiastical dignitaries active between 1800 and 1840.

Diocesan archives, usually deposited at the county record office, may include ordination papers with testimonials about a clergyman's character. Lambeth Palace Library and the Church of England Record Centre in Bermondsey (**www.lambethpalacelibrary.org**) may also hold letters written by your ancestor if he became a vicar or rector with a benefice or 'living' (ie he lived in a vicarage or rectory house owned by the Church, with an income attached). From 1704 until 1947 Queen Anne's Bounty offered financial support to poorer clergymen and plenty of interesting files survive containing correspondence about vicarages and rectories in need of repair. The file for the parish of Combe Down near Bath reveals that George W Newnham, the incumbent there from 1842 until 1877, struggled to survive on his annual salary of £53 while caring for a parish of over a thousand people who worked chiefly in local quarries, and he wrote repeatedly to Queen Anne's Bounty for assistance.

Parish records held in county record offices, or retained by the church, can provide insightful glimpses into your ancestor's relationship with their flock, and may shed more light on curates employed to support the vicar. Parish collections may consist of baptism, marriage and burial registers written in your ancestor's hand, as well as parish magazines, minutes of the parochial church council and vestry. The latter sets of records are also worth browsing if your ancestor was not a clergyman but held some other parish office like churchwarden, vestry clerk or overseer of the poor. Churchwardens and sidesmen (ushers) who served at the Cathedral and Parish Church of Manchester from 1422 through to 1911 are honoured in a book available to search on **TheGenealogist.co.uk**, held among the Occupational Records for the clergy. Peter Towey's book *My Ancestor was an Anglican Clergyman* (2006) offers further guidance for researching men who worked for the Church of England.

Detailed records about the careers of nonconformist ministers are harder to come by, since chapels were independent and funded by voluntary contributions. The county record office will be the best place to start a search for any meeting minutes, but bear in mind that ministers tended to move about frequently. Dr Williams's Centre for Dissenting Studies in London holds collections of letters, diaries and works written by prominent dissenters **(http://dwlib.co.uk)**. The John Rylands Library at the University of Manchester also holds some Methodist archives, and has an online index of ministers at **www.library.manchester.ac.uk/search-resources/guide-to-special-collections/methodist/using-the-collections/index-of-methodist-ministers/**. There is a detailed guide to the library's Methodist collections at **www.library.manchester.ac.uk/media/services/library/deansgate/methodist-guide/Guide-to-Methodist-Resources-at-The-University-of-Manchester.pdf**. The Library of the Society of Friends in Euston contains material about the history of the Quakers, and its staff can advise on surviving records for both male and female ministers **(see http://quakerstrongrooms.org/about/)**.

Medical professions

The Church used to be responsible for licensing physicians who diagnosed patients, for surgeons who performed operations, and apothecaries who prepared and sold medicines. Bishops' registers of licences held in County Record Offices record the names of medics licensed to work within the diocese during the 16th to 18th centuries. Wallis & Wallis's publication *Eighteenth Century Medics* (1988) contains a useful list of around 80,000 practitioners extracted from bishops' licences and apprenticeship registers at The National Archives (the latter are available on **TheGenealogist.co.uk**, as described in Chapter 2). Wallis & Wallis's list includes midwives, apothecaries, dentists, surgeons and physicians.

The Royal College of Physicians was founded in 1518 and records of past members are in its London library (**www.rcplondon.ac.uk/resources/library**). Munk's Roll of published biographies for licentiates of the college from 1518 to 1825 and fellows up to the present day is online at **http://munksroll.rcplondon.ac.uk**. The biographies are often very detailed, providing the physician's father's name and occupation, details of their university education, date of college admission and history of their practice. The RCP has a handy glossary at **http://munksroll.rcplondon.ac.uk/Home/Glossary** for interpreting abbreviations commonly found after a medical ancestor's name, such as 'MD' standing for Doctor of Medicine.

Apothecaries studied the effects of herbs and spices on the body. The Society of Apothecaries was incorporated in 1617, and maintains an archive at the Apothecaries' Hall in London relating to apothecaries and their assistants (**see www.apothecaries.org/the-archives/family-history**). The Royal Pharmaceutical Society founded in 1841 is more likely to hold records of chemists, druggists and pharmacists (go to **www.rpharms.com/museum-pdfs/tracing-people-and-premises-in-pharmacy.pdf**). The London Metropolitan Archives holds some copies of the Society of Apothecaries' records and has produced a research guide for tracing apothecaries, surgeons, physicians and other medical practitioners at **www.cityoflondon.gov.uk/things-to-do/london-metropolitan-archives/visitor-information/Documents/37-tracing-medical-practitioners.pdf**.

Until the 18th century barbers worked part-time as surgeons and dentists, both professions requiring a skilled hand with a blade. The Age of Enlightenment saw surgeons experiment with new techniques to advance their anatomical knowledge, and encouraged university-led learning. In 1745 the Worshipful Company of Barber-Surgeons divided in two, and in 1800 the Surgeon's Company was superseded by the Royal College of Surgeons. The college library and archive in Lincoln's Inn holds information about past members and has obituaries for 8000 fellows from 1843 through to the 21st century at **http://livesonline.rcseng.ac.uk**. The college archivist is happy to field family history enquiries about former surgeons and contact details will be found at **www.rcseng.ac.uk/museums/archives**.

The *Medical Register* has been published annually since 1859 when all practitioners needed to register with a new General Medical Council established by the British Medical Association. The even older *Medical Directory*, including the 1895 volume that is word-searchable on **TheGenealogist.co.uk**, also offers lists of physicians, surgeons, GPs and dentists practising across the country (a separate *Dentists' Register* appeared in the late 19th century), giving their addresses, qualifications, places of education, appointments and details of their published works. Included in the list on TheGenealogist.co.uk is Britain's first fully qualified female doctor, Elizabeth Garrett Anderson, who gained her MD degree in Paris in 1870. A member of the British Medical Association, in 1895 Garrett Anderson was a consultant physician at the New Hospital for Women, a lecturer and dean at the London School of Medicine for Women, and had worked at the East London Children's Hospital. The *Medical Directory* has been published every year since 1845 and includes lists of medical officers in the naval, military and Indian services, which supplements the digital Roll of Army Medical Staff also on TheGenealogist.co.uk, covering 1727 to 1898.

The *Medical Directory* of 1895, listing Britain's first fully qualified female doctor

The Wellcome Library on Euston Road in London holds extensive collections of the directories described above, plus biographical dictionaries, medical journals that include practitioners' obituaries, duplicates of bishops' licences and personal papers deposited by doctors. The library has an online catalogue and research guides, including one for researching health professionals at **http://wellcomelibrary.org/collections/archive-guides/health-professions/** containing advice about records for midwives, nurses and health visitors.

The National Archives holds some records of nurses and midwives from the late 19th century, described at **www.nationalarchives. gov.uk/help-with-your-research/research-guides/patients-doctors-nurses/**. It has also improved the catalogue of Royal Navy Medical Officers' journals so that they can be searched by the name of the surgeon (see **www.nationalarchives.gov.uk/surgeonsatsea/**). The National Archives' Ministry of Health correspondence registers contain information about cases dealt with by workhouse nurses, matrons and medical officers employed by the Poor Law authorities, and supplement the Board of Guardians' records held in county record offices.

Public services

The Civil Service was radically reformed in the 1850s, when it began recruiting well-educated people selected for their academic and professional merits rather than their family connections. The Civil Service Commission was established in 1855 to oversee the new system of examination-based recruitment, however civil servant personnel records were not generally retained. Some material may survive about employees within the records of the relevant department now deposited at The National Archives; for example, there are warrant appointments, staff lists, bills of salaries and pension records for customs officers from the 17th up to the 20th century in the CUST series, which are outlined at **www.nationalarchives.gov.uk/help-with-your-research/research-guides/customs-officers/**. The National Archives has also produced a guide to finding examination marks and results for civil service applicants, appointments to the Lord Steward's department, and other records at **www.nationalarchives.gov.uk/help-with-your-research/research-guides/civil-or-crown-servants/**.

Published lists of civil servants, such as the British Imperial Calendar (see the box opposite), are useful for finding out exactly which department an ancestor worked for, which can help lead you to the

THE IMPERIAL CALENDAR

The 1895 British Imperial Calendar and Civil Service List on **TheGenealogist.co.uk** is a fantastic resource for finding people working in a huge range of capacities, including those employed by official state departments, such as the Home Office, Foreign Office and Colonial Office, listing everyone from the Principal Secretary of State down to the doorkeeper, and those working for national, scientific and commercial institutions like the librarians, keepers and assistants at the British Museum and National Gallery. Clerks employed by the Army and Navy are listed alongside people employed by the Church and legal, medical and philanthropic institutions. The physicians, surgeons and medical officer at the Infant Orphan Asylum in Wanstead are all named, along with a brief explanation of the organisation's work taking in bereaved children from all over the Empire who were 'respectably descended', and caring for them until they reached the age of 15. The 1895 digital edition can be searched on TheGenealogist.co.uk by name, but bear in mind that first names are sometimes only initialled. Original volumes of the Imperial Calendar, which was published from 1809 to 1972, are also on open access in The National Archives' first floor reading room.

relevant records at The National Archives. Even if your ancestor's work with the British government took them overseas, the archives here in England are the best port of call. **TheGenealogist.co.uk** has a searchable copy of *Who's Who in The British War Mission in the United States*, 1918, including organisational diagrams showing the structure of each department and the ranks of the principal officers working beneath the High Commissioner. Similarly, the War Office List 1914–1921 on TheGenealogist.co.uk contains biographies for men and women working behind the scenes as typists, clerks, librarians, draughtsmen, accountants, and in a range of more senior roles.

Public office holders could be knighted for their services to Crown and Country, and the volumes of *Knights of England 1127–1904* on **TheGenealogist.co.uk** contain hundreds of entries for men in government positions. The Institute of Historical Research has compiled lists of public office holders from the 16th century up to the 19th century at **www.history.ac.uk/publications/office**, and if your ancestor worked for the Royal Household then the Royal Archives at Windsor Castle holds some records for past servants to the Crown, which are described at **www.royal.gov.uk/the%20royal%20collection%20and%20other%20collections/ theroyalarchives/theroyalarchives.aspx**.

In 1635 Charles I opened up his royal mail to the public, and in 1660 his son Charles II established the General Post Office, creating a national network of post offices and sorting stations. However the service was expensive, calculated on the distance a letter was carried until the conception of the Uniform Penny Post in 1840, which introduced pre-paid stamps. This, combined with increased literacy levels in the 19th century, meant that far more people began using the Royal Mail, and as a result more Post Office workers and letter sorters and carriers were employed. The British Postal Museum and Archive near Farringdon in London holds appointment books for people working all over the country, as well as establishment books, pension records, minute books and Post Office magazines, and has compiled a guide to resources at **www.postalheritage.org.uk/visiting/archive/genealogy/**.

Law and order

The system of policing that we rely on today emerged in England in the 19th century when Home Secretary Sir Robert Peel created the Metropolitan Police Force in 1829 to keep order in London. In 1839 the County Police Act set up a framework for regional forces.

Metropolitan Police staff and pension records are held at The National Archives in the MEPO series and record the rank, warrant number, division and dates of appointment and removal of each person. There are alphabetical registers of joiners and leavers described at **www.nationalarchives.gov.uk/help-with-your-research/research-guides/officer-in-police-force/**, and this online guide also summarises some of the police records held elsewhere. The National Archives' further guide to London Metropolitan and Transport Police at **www.nationalarchives.gov.uk/help-with-your-research/research-guides/london-metropolitan-and-transport-police/** explains the force's divisional system and points researchers to the Wapping Police Station Museum for records of ancestors who were with the Thames Division, and to the Metropolitan Police for records that it has retained (see **http://content.met.police.uk/Site/history**). The Metropolitan Police Heritage Centre next to West Brompton tube station has a database of 54,000 names dating back to 1829 (see **www.metpolicehistory.co.uk/met-police-heritage-centre.html**).

The Metropolitan Women Police Association (**www.metwpa.org.uk**) also holds the names and records for women who served from 1919 to 1986. The British Transport Police Historical Group can provide information on officers and staff employed from 1949 when the private police forces of the railway, canal and dock companies merged (see **www.btp.police.uk/about_us/our_history.aspx**).

The International Centre for the History of Crime, Policing and Justice at the Open University in Milton Keynes holds police-related journals, some documentation from various British police forces, and memoirs donated by ex-officers. Its website suggests useful resources and publications at **www.open.ac.uk/arts/research/policing/** and has a digital copy of *A Guide to the Archives of the Police Forces of England and Wales* written by Ian Bridgeman and Clive Emsley (1991), covering everywhere from the Avon and Somerset Police to Northumbria Police.

Most regional police force records are held in local archives and museums. The London Metropolitan Archives holds registers and personal files for the City of London Police from 1832, for which there is a research guide at **www.cityoflondon.gov.uk/things-to-do/london-metro-politan-archives/visitor-information/Documents/43-records-of-city-of-lond on-police-officers.pdf**. If your ancestor was responsible for enforcing the law in London then they may have given evidence at the Old Bailey. The proceedings of the Old Bailey from 1674 through to 1913 have been transcribed online and are searchable by name at **www.oldbaileyonline.org**. In May 1836 police constable Matthew Peak appeared during the trial of Dennis McDonald, indicted for stealing material from a linen drapers, and told the court that he had apprehended the prisoner in Rose and Crown Court on Sunday 27th March, taken him to the station house and gone to search his home in Christopher Square. The testimony provides his division and warrant number (G 198), which are helpful for speeding up the search for staff records in the archives.

Prior to the establishment of local police services, parish watchmen and constables were appointed to apprehend ne'er-do-wells. The Constables' Accounts of Manchester for 1612 up to 1776 on **TheGeneal-ogist.co.uk** describe in some detail the daily work carried out by constables like Benjamin L Winter and Thomas Chadwick, who on 27 October 1775 "relieved Thomas Ogden found in the streets, dying", and on 1 December confined a handful of lads at The Sun for "breaking windows and other disorders", before sending them to prison. The town's two constables were responsible for seeing to the punishment of those people accused of misdemeanours, who might be imprisoned in the dungeon, sent to the House of Correction, stood in the pillory, put in the stocks, or tied to the rogues' post where they would be whipped. The Constables' Accounts also allude to work carried out by local magistrates.

Magistrates, or Justices of the Peace, presided over summary offences at the local Petty and Quarter Sessions (replaced by Magistrates' Courts in 1971). **TheGenealogist.co.uk** has a printed return of all the Justices of the Peace (JPs) for 1911, giving their addresses, the dates of their appointment and the Petty Sessional Division to which they belonged. *Whitaker's Almanack*, an annual publication, lists staff working for metropolitan magistrates' courts. As a general rule, records of Petty and Quarter Sessions are held in the county record office. Local newspapers are also a fruitful source for details of the trials over which magistrates sat in judgement.

Judges in the higher courts of the land advised juries on 'indictable offences' heard at Assize Courts (until these were replaced by Crown Courts in 1971) and until 1964 had the power to issue the death sentence. Trials described in *The Gentleman's Magazine* and *The Annual Register* (both available at the British Library) record judges' words when sentencing prisoners. *The Biographical Dictionary of Judges of England* on **TheGenealogist.co.uk** covers 1066 to 1870 and includes an entry for Lord Chief Justice George Jeffreys who earned the accolade of the "very worst judge that ever disgraced Westminster Hall". His notoriety as the Hanging Judge stemmed from the Bloody Assizes of 1685 when he ordered the execution of at least 160 people at Taunton for their part in Monmouth's Rebellion against James II. The National Archives has produced several in-depth research guides for tracing records for the Assize Courts, Crown Courts and the myriad of other courts in England and Wales. Go to **www.nationalarchives.gov.uk/help-with-your-research/research-guides-keywords** and select 'C' for crime.

Some judges, including Jeffreys, began their legal careers as lawyers. Lawyers were historically divided into several distinct groups in England and Wales, and Stephen Wade's book *Tracing Your Legal Ancestors* (2010) contains a glossary of the various legal titles. Proctors represented ecclesiastical bodies and collegiates in the ecclesiastical courts before they were abolished in the mid-19th century. Solicitors continue to provide clients with legal advice, they instruct barristers and supervise court proceedings. Barristers are members of one of the Inns of Court in London, through which they are 'called to the Bar', and in the past they could study at one of the Inns of Chancery.

The four Inns of Court (Lincoln's Inn, Middle Temple, Inner Temple and Gray's Inn) have private libraries and archives, and volumes of admissions registers have been published and can be consulted at the British Library and other major repositories. Several historical registers are freely available online, including those for Middle Temple at **www.middletemple.org.uk/library-and-archive/archive-information-and-contacts/register-of-admissions** and Inner Temple at **www.innertemplearchives.org.uk**, plus Gray's Inn at **www.graysinn.org.uk/history/past-members** and **www.archive.org/stream/registeradmissi00inngoog#page/n5/mode/1up**.

The Law List, published annually in various guises since 1775, is the best place to look up lawyers and magistrates. The directory mentions where solicitors worked, and can be used to track any career moves and the year they stopped practising. TheGenealogist.co.uk has digital copies of the Law List for 1824, 1826 and 1856, as well as The Solicitors' Diary, Almanac and Legal Directory for 1900, containing a complete list of practising barristers and solicitors, plus other legal officers and staff serving in the many courts around the country.

The Law Society has a detailed research guide for tracing past solicitors at **www.lawsociety.org.uk/support-services/library-services/research-guides/documents/15-how-to-trace-past-solicitors-and-law-firms** and The National Archives' research guides at **www.nationalarchives.gov.uk/help-with-your-research/research-guides/lawyers/** and **www.nationalarchives.gov.uk/help-with-your-research/research-guides/lawyers-further-research/** outline additional records held at Kew. In-depth guidance can also be sought from *My Ancestor was a Lawyer* by Brian Brooks (2006) and G Holborn's *Sources of Biographical Information on Past Lawyers* (1999).

Financial services

The history of modern day British banking can be traced back to the 17th century when goldsmiths in London began safeguarding deposits, paying interest, issuing early forms of cheques and offering loans. Several long-standing banks manage their own archives, such as the Archive of Lloyds Banking Group, comprising branch records, staff registers, photographs and minute books dating back to 1695 (**www.lloydsbank-inggroup.com/our-group/our-heritage/our-archives/**). The Rothschild family of bankers descends from Mayer Amschel Rothschild, whose five sons established businesses in London, Frankfurt, Paris, Vienna and Naples during the 18th and early 19th centuries. The business records of the London branch forms the core of the Rothschild Archive in the City of London, and most papers up to 1945 are available for public consultation (**see www.rothschildarchive.org**).

The Bank of England was formed in 1694 to act as the Government's banker, raise funds for Government ventures and manage the subsequent debt. It was privately owned until being nationalised in 1946. There is an archive in the basement of the Bank of England on Threadneedle Street, London, where employment records can be consulted for former staff, and historic customer account records will be found. The archive is fully catalogued at **www.bankofengland.co.uk/archive** and digital content on the website includes service histories of clerks granted leave to serve in the Armed Forces during World War One.

If your ancestor worked as an accountant then the Institute of Chartered Accountants in England and Wales (ICAEW) guide at **www.icaew.com/en/library/historical-resources/family-history** will come in handy. The ICAEW has created the Accountancy Ancestors database containing indexes to over 7000 obituaries and biographies and thousands of photographs of accountants who were in business between 1874 and 1965. The ICAEW Library and Information Service in London holds the sources described in the database.

AVIATION

The Flying Book of 1918 on **TheGenealogist.co.uk** names administrative officers of high rank and pioneers of aviation who were in the King's service. The first page contains an entry for H W Barber; born in 1874 he was "the fourth or fifth Englishman to fly". Barber built 28 planes but gave up flying aged 38 in 1912 and became an aeronautical consultant to Lloyds, described as "practically the father of aviation insurance". TheGenealogist.co.uk also has a collection of Pilots' Certificates among its occupational records.

Military careers

Although the British Army can trace its history back to the time of the Civil War, the majority of surviving personnel records date from the 18th century onwards. Records in the public domain (i.e. dating from before 1922) are primarily held at The National Archives, and consist of pension records, campaign medals, regimental muster rolls, pay lists and some early service records for soldiers and non-commissioned officers who served with the Royal Artillery between 1755 and 1917. There is a research guide at **www.nationalarchives.gov.uk/help-with-your-research/research-guides/british-army-soldiers-up-to-1913/** for locating soldiers' records prior to the First World War, and one for pre-1914 officers' records at **www.nationalarchives.gov.uk/help-with-your-research/research-guides/british-army-officers-up-to-1913/**. Details of cadets and staff who attended the Sandhurst Academy between the early 18th century and late 20th century can also be searched at **http://archive.sandhurstcollection.co.uk/search/**. If your ancestor served with the Indian Army then there is a high chance that the British Library will hold records in its India Office collections (see **http://indiafamily.bl.uk/ui/Sources.aspx**).

The names and positions of Army and Navy officers before and after the two World Wars are collated in the annual, quarterly and monthly published Army List, the Navy List and the Air Force List, of which there are comprehensive collections on **TheGenealogist.co.uk** that can be searched by name. The lists provide dates of birth and promotions, and may include details of an officer's war service.

Senior officers were responsible for writing despatches to high command, and the writings of those who were in the regular Army and Navy when World War One erupted feature in the collection of Naval and Military Despatches that are searchable on TheGenealogist.co.uk. Vice-Admiral Sir David Beatty reported his movements on the battle-cruiser HMS Lion in great detail during the initial days of the war, during which he saw action in the first naval battle at Heligoland Bight. Officers and men were singled out for special mention in despatches, and summaries from before, during and after the war were also published in the London Gazette, along with details of promotions, which can be searched at **www.thegazette.co.uk**. Digital newspapers help to bring the WW1 period to life, and the *Illustrated War News*, *The Great War*, *The Sphere* and *War Illustrated* can all be searched by keyword or browsed page-by-page on **TheGenealogist.co.uk**.

The National Archives holds the 40% of First World War Army service records that survived the Blitz. It has comprehensive research guides to sourcing records for Army, Royal Navy, Royal Naval Air Service, Royal Marines, Royal Flying Corps and Royal Air Force personnel at **www.nationalarchives.gov.uk/help-with-your-research/research-guides-keywords/** under 'A' and 'R'.

The Ministry of Defence retains service records of ancestors who served with any of the Armed Forces after WW1. Records are released to next of kin upon request after paying a fee and providing a copy of the person's death certificate. There are instructions on how to apply at **www.gov.uk/guidance/requests-for-personal-data-and-service-records#service-records-of-deceased-service-personnel**. Some operational records for the post-war period will be found at The National Archives, including war diaries and Operational Record Books of the RAF (see **www.nationalarchives.gov.uk/help-with-your-research/research-guides/raf-operations-record-books-1939-1945/**), but investigating your ancestor's personnel records should be the first step. William Spencer's books *Army Records* (2008), *Family History in the Wars* (2007) and *Air Force Records for Family Historians* (2008) are the authoritative texts on this subject, as well as Bruno Pappalardo's guide to *Tracing Your Naval Ancestors* (2003).

Many records can illuminate the lives of tradespeople in the past

Chapter Five: Profit & Loss

I n this chapter we take a look at collections of records that are worth investigating to chart the peaks and troughs in your ancestor's career, whether they were tradespeople, craftspeople, businessmen, mariners, military men or labourers.

Wills and probate

Wills are one of the most informative sources when it comes to measuring how successful your ancestor was in business, providing an idea of how wealthy they were based on the sums and belongings they bequeathed to loved ones. The National Archives has a handy old-to-new money converter at **www.nationalarchives.gov.uk/currency/** to gauge how much your ancestor's estate would be worth in the 21st century. Wills often provide the names of associates and indicate whether any relatives inherited a family firm.

Before 1858 hundreds of ecclesiastical courts across the country administered probate cases, giving executors the necessary authority to carry out the deceased's wishes. The Prerogative Court of Canterbury (PCC) usually dealt with the wills of the wealthiest testators (ie deceased will makers) and those with assets situated in more than one diocese in the south of England. Over a million digital copies of PCC wills proved between 1384 and 1858 can be searched by name and profession on **TheGenealogist.co.uk**. The will of draper John Living of Chertsey, Surrey, written in 1777 and proved upon his death in 1782 (see overleaf), left his real and personal estate in trust with merchant Thomas Dunn, with instructions to have his stock appraised and to allow his wife Ann to carry on his trade "for the support of herself and family".

The PCC did not only administer the estates of business owners and the excessively wealthy – we also find the wills of female weavers, miners and even labourers in the collection on TheGenealogist.co.uk. The wills of people who died overseas were always proved by the PCC, and so the 1813 will of John Shepherd is there, described as a mariner lately on His Majesty's Ship La Minerve, but "now a Prisoner of War at the depot of Givet in France", having been captured during the Napoleonic Wars.

The Prerogative Court of York mirrored the work of the PCC in the north of England. Wills proved there from the 14th century to the mid 19th century are now held at the Borthwick Institute in York, which has

The will of draper John Living of Chertsey, Surrey, written in 1777

developed a research guide on the subject at **www.york.ac.uk/borthwick/holdings/guides/research-guides/probate-courts/**. A partial index is available on TheGenealogist.co.uk for 1389 to 1652, listed under 'Yorkshire Wills' and taken from the York Registry.

If your ancestor's will was not proved by one of the Archbishops' Prerogative Courts then it could have been taken to the local Archdeacon's Court, or to the Bishop's Consistory or Commissary Court if their property was scattered across more than one archdeaconry. The records of these courts are usually found among diocesan records at the County Record Office, and J Gibson's book *Probate Jurisdictions: Where to Look for Wills* (2002) offers a comprehensive guide to each court and also deals with 'peculiar' jurisdictions. Wills proved in ecclesiastical courts in Wales prior to 1858 can be searched on the National Library of Wales catalogue at **cat.llgc.org.uk/probate**.

On 11th January 1858 a National Probate Calendar was set up for England and Wales and a new civil probate court system replaced the complicated network of ecclesiastical courts. District probate registries were established across the country, with a Principal Probate Registry in London to which copies of wills registered at all the district offices were sent. There is an online database of all wills proved in England and Wales from 1858 to the present at **https://probatesearch.service.gov.uk/#wills** through which you can order digital copies.

If your ancestor did not write a will, but next-of-kin needed permission from the court to process the estate, then Letters of Administration were granted, hence the word 'Administration' or 'Admon' might be found next to an ancestor's name in probate indexes. This means that a will does not exist.

Death duty needed to be paid on estates over a certain value from 1796 until 1906 when it was superseded by Inheritance Tax, though very few death duty records survive after 1903. Death duty registers list all liable estates, and surviving records are held at The National Archives. They record the date and place of death, the value of the deceased's personal estate, details of people due to inherit from the estate, and they were sometimes updated in later years to include the dates of marriage or death of any beneficiaries, births of children and grandchildren, changes of address and references to any law suits. The National Archives has an in-depth research guide at **www.nationalarchives.gov.uk/help-with-your-research/research-guides/country-court-death-duty-registers-1796-1811/** with details about how to find entries in the registers.

Success stories

If your ancestor achieved great things then there is every chance they are mentioned in the Oxford Dictionary of National Biography or a biographical dictionary dedicated to their field of work. The Biography & Who's Who section on **TheGenealogist.co.uk** includes a copy of the *Oxford Dictionary of National Biography* covering 1654–1930 and also *The Imperial Dictionary of Universal Biography* pertaining to "writers of eminence in the various branches of literature, science and art". Included in the latter is an entry for the celebrated court musician Joah Bates (c1740/1–1799). Bates evidently had more than one string to his bow and was appointed Commissioner of the Victualling Office and an official on the Board of Customs during the era when nepotism in the Civil Service was par for the course.

Obituaries for people in high office are likely to be found in national newspapers, which can be searched in the British Library's News Room (**www.bl.uk/collection-guides/newspapers**). Tributes to local dignitaries were published in regional newspapers, copies of which can be found in local archives and also in the national collection at the British Library. The *Illustrated London News* available on *TheGenealogist.co.uk* contains mid 19th-century birth, marriage and death announcements for influential professionals, as well as columns dedicated to military and naval intelligence, church and university news, with details of promotions awarded, and law reports.

Articles in the *Illustrated London News* also elucidate the low points in our ancestors' careers. Summaries of proceedings in the Central Criminal Court in 1842 noted the trial of Post Office letter carrier William Taylor, aged 24, who was charged with having stolen a letter containing half a sovereign. Taylor pleaded not guilty at first, but later changed his plea to guilty. Though several respectable witnesses testified to his excellent character for honesty, and it was acknowledged that he had been in great distress after a recent bout of illness, the court sentenced him to two years' hard labour.

Insurance against disaster

Fire was a constant threat to businesses, particularly those with timber-built premises. Specialist fire insurance companies thrived following the Great Fire of London in 1666, which started in a bakery. Even after laws were passed to ensure that all new buildings were built of brick or stone, businesses were still susceptible. Albion Mills, a substantial building erected on the south side of Blackfriars Bridge in 1786, was completely gutted by fire just five years after it opened. *The Imperial Dictionary of Universal Biography* notes that Joah Bates had invested both his and his wife's entire savings in the Albion Mills venture. The couple were completely ruined by its conflagration.

Many fire insurance companies were based in London and the records of around 80 companies are held at the London Metropolitan Archives, including registers of policies purchased by customers. There are some indexes to the registers, including an index for Royal and Sun Alliance policy registers dating from the late 18th century to the mid 19th century on the online catalogue at **www.cityoflondon.gov.uk/things-to-do/london-metropolitan-archives/Pages/search.aspx**. Using the online index alone it is evident that fishing tackle maker Benjamin Chevalier insured his premises at 12 Bell Yard in London from at least 1797 until 1833, and that Thomas Bowness had taken over Chevalier's tackle shop by 1838. Another index to over 160,000 policies issued by the Sun and Royal Exchange between 1777 and 1786 can be searched at **www.londonlives.org/static/AHDSFIR.jsp**. The London Metropolitan Archives' lengthy research guide points to further microfiche indexes at **www.cityoflondon.gov.uk/things-to-do/london-metropolitan-archives/visitor-information/Documents/48-fire-insurance-records.pdf**.

Charles E Goad Ltd specialised in producing fire insurance maps and plans for major towns and cities. The first plans were drawn up in the 1870s, and are colour-coded and annotated with symbols to indicate how each building was used, the height of buildings and the materials from which they were constructed. The names of companies operating from commercial premises are written onto the maps, and several updated editions were produced for some areas. The British Library owns all Goad maps published nationally between 1895 and 1924, though collections may also be found in local archives up to the 1970s. See Goad's *A Catalogue of Fire Insurance Plans Published by Chas E Goad 1878–1970* (1984) for a full overview.

Insurance records are also pertinent to researching ancestors who had stakes in merchant shipping. Lloyds of London emerged as a specialist in marine insurance, originating in Edward Lloyd's coffee house in the 1680s. The Guildhall Library in London houses part of the company's archive, consisting of the *Lloyd's List* newspaper published from 1740 and original archive documents recording ships' captains, details of voyages and casualty reports, records of marine losses and war losses, and Board of Trade inquiries. Declan Barriskill's *Guide to the Lloyd's Marine Collection* (1994) is the definitive handbook for accessing the records and there is an online summary sheet at **www.lr.org/en/_images/213-35632_03-guildhall.pdf**.

World War One claim settlements for marine War Risks Insurance held at The National Archives also offer up a surprising amount of information about the commercial activities of all types of companies that shipped goods around the globe despite the risk of submarine attack. For example R H Green was awarded £1040 for the loss of cattle that went down with the Alnwick Castle, torpedoed in March 1917 en route from Plymouth to Cape Town. The records, held in series BT 365, have been catalogued in great detail so they can be searched by company name at **http://discovery.nationalarchives.gov.uk**.

A large number of compensation claims were made against the Sheffield Water Company by cutlers, manufacturers and local businesses affected by a flash flood when the Dale Dyke Dam burst on 11 March 1864, killing 250 people and causing widespread damage. James Crossland, miller of Don Mills, claimed over £223 for bags of damaged flour, oatmeal, bran and wheat, a wheelbarrow, coal and pigs that were carried away by the torrent, and the cost of labour and lost time in cleaning the mill, offices and machinery. The Sheffield Flood Claims Archive can be searched by name at **www2.shu.ac.uk/sfca**, where there are full transcriptions of the original material held at Sheffield Archives.

The British Insurance Business, 1547–1970: A Guide to its History and Records by Cockerell and Green (1994) covers all types of insurance archives held across the country, including the Phoenix Assurance records held by Cambridge University Library.

Debt and dissolution

Ancestors who got into financial difficulties could declare themselves bankrupt if they were traders who bought and sold goods (though in reality many people who were not true traders also declared bankruptcy). Individuals who racked up debts on credit that they couldn't afford to repay were termed 'insolvent debtors', and up to 1869 they could be left to languish in a debtors' prison until their creditors had been repaid, sometimes achieved through the sale of property.

A list of bankrupts from 1786 to 1806 is available to search on **TheGenealogist.co.uk**, giving details of the companies' dividends and the name and address of the company's solicitor, which could be useful to

DISPUTES

Legal disputes concerning property and money, including actions against bankrupts, could be brought before the Court of Chancery. Pleadings and evidence were gathered, and although few cases were ever fully resolved, a large amount of paperwork generated by the court survives at The National Archives. **TheGenealogist.co.uk** has an index to Chancery Proceedings from c1377 to 1714, from which we learn that John Rose brought a case against John Thompson and others concerning Merton water mills in 1674. The National Archives has devised in-depth research guides to penetrating the original records within this complex record set at **www.nationalarchives.gov.uk/help-with-your-research/research-guides/ chancery-equity-suits-after-1558/** and **www.nationalarchives.gov.uk/help-with-your-research/research-guides/chancery-cases-supreme-court-after-1875/**.

tracking down further business records. The official government gazettes published regular notices of bankrupts and insolvent debtors, which can be searched by name at **www.thegazette.co.uk**. The *London Gazette* noted that William Coupe of South Shoebury in Essex who was a chemist, druggist, newsagent and stationer who also carried on business in Brentwood, was declared bankrupt in August 1866. Further information about his plight might be found in the local archives and also at The National Archives, which holds some original records for bankrupts and insolvent debtors. There is a research guide at **www.nationalarchives.gov.uk/help-with-your-research/research-guides/bankrupts-insolvent-debtors/** for navigating the sample of surviving bankruptcy case files, bankruptcy proceedings registers, appeals and registers of petitions to the Court for the Relief of Insolvent Debtors.

The gazettes not only contain notices of bankruptcies, but like The Times they also advertise the dissolution of partnerships and businesses that had ceased trading. Some local libraries offer free home access to The Times Digital Archive. Winding-up files for a sample of companies dissolved after 1860 are held at The National Archives in series BT 31. They often include lists shareholders, annual returns, articles of association, registers of directors and other legal paperwork. Series BT 41 contains similar records for Joint Stock Companies dissolved between 1841 and 1860, and both series can be searched by company name using the online catalogue at **http://discovery.nationalarchives.gov.uk**.

Seeking relief

The records of local Poor Law authorities can give real insight into the employment history of ancestors who couldn't financially support themselves or their families because they were unable to find regular work. Those at the lower level of society were the most vulnerable, including labourers from all employment sectors.

In 1834 the New Poor Law overhauled a system of relief that had been little changed since Elizabethan times. The so-called Old Poor Law was administered by parish authorities and established a system of workhouses opened on a voluntary basis and paid for through local rates. Paupers could apply for 'out relief' prior to the Victorian period, so that they didn't have to go into the workhouse. The New Poor Law embodied a changing attitude to the poor, who were increasingly viewed as idle. It enforced a standardised, centralised network of workhouses administered by Boards of Guardians, who did away with out relief to deter claimants.

The types of records that survive locally vary. If you are looking for paupers prior to 1834 then records will be held in parish collections at the local County Record Office. After 1834 Poor Law Unions were set up, so that paupers from several neighbouring parishes applied to one union. The website **www.workhouses.org.uk** contains lots of information about the way individual workhouses and Poor Law authorities operated across the country. In most cases you can hope to find admission and discharge records (often arranged chronologically); creed records that are usually arranged alphabetically and are useful as a first port of call to establish when an ancestor was admitted to the workhouse; settlement papers proving why a pauper was entitled to relief in the parish where they were applying; removal papers in cases where paupers were sent to their parish of origin to apply for relief. More detailed information might survive in the form of petitions for relief and other miscellaneous papers created by the overseer or Board of Guardians.

The Assistant Overseer of the City of London Poor Law Authority made enquiries about those seeking relief in his union in the mid Victorian period, and a register of the questions he asked and answers he received survives at the London Metropolitan Archives. In October 1849 he visited the ex-employer of Martin Welsh of 5 Green Court to enquire whether it was true that Welsh had fallen from a ladder some weeks since and was unable to work, and asked whether it was likely he would be employed at Mr Trago's again. The reply was in the affirmative from Mr Trago, and further enquiries with Mrs Welsh revealed that her husband left London in search of work 3 weeks ago, and though she didn't know where he was, she was in daily expectation of receiving some money from him. This depth of information is unlikely to be found anywhere else.

Migration in search of work was more common than we might expect and people could travel great distances and even settle in another country, so it's worth widening the net if your ancestors disappear from the area where you're expecting to find them. Colonies of Cornish miners travelled all the way to Argentina, Mexico, Brazil, Australia, New Zealand, Canada, the United States and South Africa when the Cornish mining industry declined in the 19th century.

A passenger list at TheGenealogist showing a group of miners travelling to Australia

Workers who set sail from the UK to ports outside of Europe in the late 19th century and early 20th century can be found in ships' passenger lists, which have recently been added to **TheGenealogist.co.uk**.

The website also has collections of international records from America, Australia, India, New Zealand, South Africa and other countries so you can continue to trace ancestors after they settled in those countries.

It wasn't always feasible or affordable to take the whole family away. Money might be sent back home, but again Poor Law records can reveal the reason for a family being left dependent on the state for support. Weaver Hall Museum and Workhouse in Cheshire and The Workhouse in Southwell, Nottinghamshire, portray life in these dismal institutions, and it's easy to see why no one would want to stay longer than necessary. Financial difficulties and fear of the workhouse might therefore explain an unexpected change in your ancestor's occupation.

In the next chapter we look at entertainers, who often needed to juggle jobs to make ends meet.

Mrs Lillie Langtry as Mrs Hardcastle in She Stoops to Conquer

Chapter Six: Entertainers

The 1891 census recorded more than 48,000 people working in the theatre, music and the arts. The late Victorian period saw a proliferation of new entertainment venues, as bawdy music halls with rowdy variety shows jostled for custom, competing with the older established theatres. Perhaps your ancestor chose to follow their heart rather than chase the money. Stories about ancestors who ran off with the circus can be hard to prove, but this chapter explores how to find out if your ancestor made a name for themselves in the entertainment industry.

The stage

Theatre evolved from religious open-air plays in the medieval period to providing courtly entertainment during the Elizabethan Age when playhouses started to open. Theatre companies were licensed for the first time and writers such as William Shakespeare came to prominence, who in turn made actors including Richard Burbage famous. Seventeenth-century Puritans frowned on the frivolity of play-acting, however. Oliver Cromwell's contemporary William Prynne denounced actresses as "notorious whores", and theatres were closed during the Civil War. They reopened in spectacular fashion after the restoration of Charles II to the throne, and the king encouraged female parts to be played by professional actresses rather than boys. It is little surprise then that the actress Nell Gwyn became his mistress, bearing him two illegitimate children.

The works of some of the most celebrated performers and writers prior to the early 19th century are described in *Biographia Dramatica* and can be searched by name on **TheGenealogist.co.uk**. The biographies elaborate on romantic partnerships formed within theatrical circles. Included is an entry for C Macartney, a provincial actor who wrote a comic opera entitled The Vow and performed at Birmingham in 1800, "where, after a short courtship, he married Miss Minton, aged 15, who was then

WHO'S WHO

TheGenealogist.co.uk has several biographical volumes that can be searched by name for people in the entertainment business, including *Biographia Dramatica; Who's Who in The Theatre,* 1922; *Who's Who in Music,* 1935; and *Who's Who in Sport,* 1935. You can search all volumes at once using the Master Search.

performing with the company". Women were usually expected to give up an acting career upon marriage, though exceptions could be made if their husband was also in the business.

The theatre gradually gained respectability in the 19th century, though actresses in particular continued to be the focus of salacious gossip columns. Mrs Lillie Langtry's relationship with the Prince of Wales (later Edward VII) was an open secret. However this indiscretion and her subsequent affairs with a string of powerful men are not the subject of her biographical entry in *Who's Who in the Theatre*, 1922, which focuses on her many stage credits and successful career as a producer. This book is available on **TheGenealogist.co.uk** and names the theatres and companies that each actor worked with, providing an in-road to archival records.

LAN] WHO'S WHO IN THE THEATRE [LAN

Taming of the Shrew," Bardelys in " Bardelys the Magnificent," King Charles in " Sweet Nell of Old Drury," Macbeth, Hamlet, Shylock, Romeo, Benedick, The Stranger in " The Passing of the Third Floor Back " ; Othello and Don Caesar in " A Royal Rival " ; at Cape Town, Oct. 1911, played the title *rôle* in " Jack o' Jingles " ; the tour was highly successful ; subsequently he sailed for India and the Far East, where he was equally successful ; re-appeared in London, at the Palladium, Feb., 1913, as Amyas Leigh in " Westward Ho ! " ; at His Majesty's, Apr., 1913, played Charles Surface in " The School for Scandal " ; at the Strand, July, 1913, appeared as 'Poleon Doret in " The Barrier " ; Nov., 1913, scored a great success when he appeared as Wu Li Chang in " Mr. Wu " ; at His Majesty's, Nov., 1914, played Henry Percy (Hotspur) in " King Henry IV " (Part I) ; subsequently, in 1915, toured as Mr. Wu and as Gringoire in " The Ballad Monger " ; at the Aldwych, July, 1915, re-appeared as Pete in the play of that name ; he then toured with his own company, and at Wimbledon, Sept., 1915, played Shylock in " The Merchant of Venice," appearing at the St. James's, under his own management, Dec., 1915, in the same part ; at the Gaiety, Hastings, Apr., 1916, played Henry Harford in " The Mystery of John Wake " ; he then appeared at the Strand, Nov., 1916, as Henri Buxell in " Buxell," and Jan., 1917, as Stephen Denby in " Under Cover " ; entered on the management of the Lyric Theatre, July, 1918, when he played the Comte de Trevières in his own adaptation " The Purple Mask " ; entered on the management of the New Theatre, Feb., 1920, when he played Silvio Steno in " Carnival," of which he was also part-author with H. C. M. Hardinge ; in the same month, for a series of matinées, also appeared as Othello ; at the New, Sept., 1920, appeared as Matathias in " The Wandering Jew," which ran twelve months. *Favourite part :* Hamlet. *Hobbies :* Art and literature, and sailing. *Club :* Green Room. *Address :* 11 Gerrard Street, W.1. *Telephone No. :* Regent 2920.

LANGTRY, Lillie, actress ; *b.* Jersey, 13 Oct., 1852 ; *d.* of Very Rev. W. C. E. le Breton, Dean of Jersey ; *m.* (1) Edward Langtry (died 1897) ; (2) Sir (then Mr.) Hugo de Bathe, Bart. ; made her first appearance on the stage, at the Haymarket Theatre, 15 Dec., 1881, under Mr. and Mrs. Bancroft, as Kate Hardcastle in " She Stoops to Conquer " ; subsequently appeared at the same theatre, as Blanche Haye in " Ours " ; organised her own company and played a season at the Imperial, Sept., 1882, playing Hester Grazebrook in " An Unequal Match," and Rosalind in " As You Like It " ; toured in America with great success ; on returning to London, became manageress of the Prince's Theatre, opening in Jan., 1885, as Séverine in " Princess George " ; in Feb., 1885, played there as Lady Teazle in " The School for Scandal " ; and Apr., 1885, as Lady Ormond in a revival of " Peril " ; at the same theatre, Jan., 1886, appeared as Margaret Glenn in " Enemies," subsequently playing Pauline in " The Lady of Lyons " ; returned to America, and played there until 1889 ; returning to England, she toured the English provinces ; assumed the management of the St. James's, Feb., 1890, reviving " As You Like It " ; in May, 1890, appeared as Esther Sandraz in the play of that name ; assumed the management of the Princess's Theatre, Nov., 1890, opening as Cleopatra in a revival of " Antony and Cleopatra " ; in Feb., 1891, produced " Lady Barter," and in Apr., 1891, " Linda Grey " ; subsequently made further American and provincial tours ; re-appeared in London, at the Grand, Islington, June, 1895, as Mrs. Barry in " Gossip," appearing in the same part at the Comedy, in the following year ; produced " The Degenerates," at the Haymarket, Aug., 1899, playing the part of Mrs. Trevelyan, with great success ; opened the rebuilt Imperial Theatre, Apr., 1901, of which she took a long lease, with the production of " A Royal Necklace " ; Jan., 1902, produced " Mademoiselle Mars," in which she appeared in the title *rôle* ; at the same theatre, Dec., 1902, played Virginia, Duchess of Keensbury in " The

475

Lillie Langtry's entry in *Who's Who in the Theatre*, 1922

The archives of theatrical companies, performers and private collectors are preserved in a range of special collections around the country, and it's worth checking all relevant catalogues for a document trail since there is no hard and fast rule about what material is stored where.

The Victoria & Albert Museum's Theatre and Performance Collection represents one of the largest holdings, containing diaries, letters, manuscripts, ephemera, business papers, designs and photographs. Plays licensed through the Lord Chamberlain's office up to the end of censorship in 1968 are documented, and over half a million playbills have been saved, which name the stars of each show. The Theatre and Performance Collection can be searched using the V&A online catalogues listed at **www.vam.ac.uk/content/articles/t/archives-theatre-performance** and there is a range of subject guides at **www.vam.ac.uk/page/t/theatre-and-performance/**.

The University of Bristol's Theatre Collection covers the period from 1572 to the present day. Its holdings are varied, and among the highlights are programmes, playbills and photos from the Bath Theatre Royal and the archive of the Bristol Old Vic Company. The catalogue at **www.bristol.ac.uk/theatrecollection/search/** includes a People Search form for finding records of actors, directors, designers, composers and playwrights who worked all over the country.

The Garrick Club, founded in 1831 as a meeting place for actors and literary men, maintains a library to which thousands of plays, manuscripts, prints and photographs have been donated documenting the history of theatre in the 18th and 19th centuries. There is an almost complete collection of playbills for the Theatres Royal on Drury Lane and Covent Garden from 1748 to 1840. Appointments can be made to visit the library and there is further information at **www.garrickclub.co.uk/library/**.

Local studies libraries and county record offices are also worth checking for material about provincial performances. The Leeds Playbills site at **www.leodis.net/playbills/** covers from 1781 up to the 1990s, and Plymouth Library Service has a webpage dedicated to the city's theatre heritage at **www.plymouth.gov.uk/homepage/leisureandtourism/libraries/whatsinyourlibrary/lns/theatrehistory.htm**.

Collections in the National Resource Centre for Dance (NRCD) Archive at the University of Surrey include the records of theatrical dance associations and societies, documents deposited by dance companies and private individuals' papers, and are described in more detail at **www.surrey.ac.uk/nrcd/archives/**.

HEADING FOR BROADWAY

Dramatic acts that did well in London's West End inevitably travelled across the Atlantic to try their luck on Broadway. Outbound ships' passenger lists on **TheGenealogist.co.uk** cover 1896 to 1909 and include the voyage of the SS Minnehaha travelling from London to New York in October 1901. Amongst the cabin passengers was theatre manager Sir Henry Irving, the first actor to be awarded a knighthood, accompanied by a troupe of 'theatricals', actors and actresses, including the famous Ellen Terry. Musicians who were employed to entertain during a voyage can also be found in ships' passenger lists. Bandsman Wallace Hartley appears on the list for the ill-fated Titanic, which can be searched at the same site. The band was widely reported to have kept playing to the bitter end. Another ship famed for its gigantic proportions, the SS Great Britain, launched its own weekly newspaper for passengers in 1865. The *SS Great Britain Times* was published under the slogan 'amusement to all – offence to none!' and advertised the programme of concerts set to take place in 'The Great Britain Music Hall' aboard the ship designed by Isambard Kingdom Brunel. The names of concert singers and passengers can be searched on TheGenealogist.co.uk, where the paper can also be browsed page-by-page.

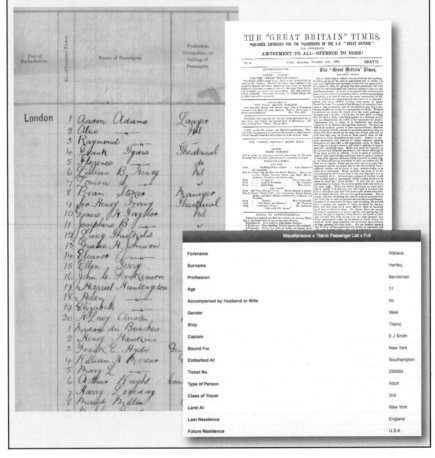

Local newspapers and specialist journals are invaluable for finding advertisements for shows and critical reviews, since they often name principal actors and producers. The *Illustrated London News* is available to search on **TheGenealogist.co.uk** right the way through from 1842 to 1889 and offers reams of columns dedicated to London's playhouses. Readers of *Harper's Magazine* also enjoyed features about antics on the stage. An issue from 1889 that is searchable on **TheGenealogist.co.uk** reflects on a century of *Hamlet,* complete with portraits of some of the key players who brought Shakespeare's prince to life throughout the 19th century. Several journals dedicated to dramatic content can be consulted in the British Library News Room at St Pancras, including *The Era* published from 1838 to 1939, the *Theatrical Journal* published from 1839 to 1873, and *The Stage* founded in 1880 and still in circulation today. For further advice, try *My Ancestor Worked in Theatre* by Alan Ruston (2005).

Captured on camera

Actors and comics at the turn of the last century began to play with the possibilities of film. The first motion picture cameras were invented in the 1890s, and their potential for the entertainment industry was quickly recognised. In little more than a decade filmmakers helped to propel the first film stars to international fame.

The British Library holds directories for those people formerly involved in the film industry, and its Moving Image Collections include silent films and thousands of television programmes. Learn more about the 70,000 items in the collection at **www.bl.uk/reshelp/find helprestype/movingimage/movingimagecoll/**. The British Film Institute (BFI) National Archive established in 1935 is one of the largest collectors in the world of films and television programmes. It has an online catalogue and guides to accessing material at **www.bfi.org.uk/archive-collections**. The BFI offers viewing services for BBC visual productions, but the BBC Written Archives holds separate correspondence about production staff, contributors and contracted performers, plus historical publications of the Radio Times. The archive is in Reading and further information will be found at **www.bbc.co.uk/historyofthebbc/research/wac**.

There is a network of regional archives that are particularly useful for locating television footage if your ancestor worked for one of the major regional broadcasters launched since the mid 20th century. Among the member bodies of Film Archives UK are the East Anglian Film Archive that holds productions by Anglia Television and BBC East (www.eafa.org.uk), the Media Archive for Central England, which has received a large collection of regional television programmes donated by ITV (www.macearchive.org), and the South West Film and Television Archive (http://swfta.co.uk).

The National Media Museum in Bradford looks after 3.5 million historically significant items in the National Television, National Cinematography and National Photography Collections, which are described at www.nationalmediamuseum.org.uk/Collection.aspx. The latter includes over 3 million photographs from the Daily Herald newspaper archive, and thousands more acquired from the Royal Photographic Society.

If your ancestor was a photographer, you may find details of their studio advertised in local trade directories on TheGenealogist.co.uk. This artistic profession appealed to women as much as men. Mrs Emily Kate Kingham of 7 Cauldwell Street in Bedford listed her photographic services in *Kelly's Bedfordshire Directory* of 1903 (see below). Further searches in annual trade directories confirm that she traded between 1890 and 1914, having taken over her husband Henry's business in the 1880s. The 1901 census reveals that the widow employed at least one male photographer who boarded at her home studio.

| DIRECTORY.] | BEDFORDSHIRE. | BEDFORD. 63 |

Hulatt George, carpenter & joiner, 23 Chandos street
Hulks Jane (Mrs.), apartments, 28 Ombersley road
Hull William, wardrobe dealer, 14 Gwyn street
Humphreys Edwin, Commercial tavern P.H. 35 Commercial rd
Humphrey Eliza Jane (Mrs.), dress maker, 107 Howbury street
Humphreys Frederick, beer retailer, 6 Ford End road
Humphreys George, hatter, 6 Bromham road
Humphreys Thomas, umbrella maker, 1 Hassett street
Humphreys William Henry, grocer, 17 Princes street
Hunt Joshua William, district manager Eastman's Limited, 111 Castle street
Hurman Walter, cabinet maker, 48 Castle hill
Hutchings George, painter, 2 Melbourne street
Hutley Simeon, boot maker, 63 Queen street
Hutton Emily (Mrs.), baker & confectioner, 129 Midland road
Hyde Ishmael Amos, insurance agent, Hartington street
Ibbett George, boot maker, 159 Tavistock street
Ibbott Arthur, builder, 1 Cardington road
Ibbott Charles, dairyman, 39 St. Peter's street
Impey James Henry, dairyman, 14 St. John's street
Inch James W. steward Bedford Club & Bowling Green Co. Limited, 9 De Pary's avenue
Ingram Alice (Mrs.), householder, 13 St. Minver road
Ingram Maurice, grocer, 69 Tavistock street
Ingram Maurice F. grocer & sub-postmaster, 25 Castle road
Ingrey Edward, confectioner, 17 Millbrook road
Inland Revenue Office (Francis Mulligan, supervisor; Caleb Killick & Thomas Hannam, officers), 1A, St. Paul's square
Inskip Ernest Henry Caleb, surveyor to the Kempston Urban District Council, Castle road east
International Tea Company's Stores Lim. (Percy Charles Bailey, manager), 84 High street
Irving William, shopkeeper, 78 Russell street
Irwin Caroline (Mrs.), householder, 22 Castle road
Isitt James Edwin, wool merchant, Union Bank chambers, St. Paul's square
Ison William Edward, gold & silver smith, see John Bull & Co
Ives Aaron, beer retailer & furniture dealer, 34 Cauldwell street
Ives Annie (Mrs.), wardrobe dealer, 143 Tavistock street
Ives Job, Shoulder of Mutton P.H. 10 Midland road
Ivett Elizabeth Ann (Mrs.), Wrestlers' inn, 4 St. Cuthbert's st
Ivin John, chief clerk of the county police, Shire hall, St. Paul's square
Izzard & Sons, plumbers, 100 Bromham road
Izzard Alfred, house decorator, 26 Park road west
Jackson Elizabeth (Miss), apartments, 19 Foster Hill road
Jackson Esau Clark, Queen's Head P.H. 38 Kempston road
Jackson John Atkinson, costumier, 98 High street
Jacobs & Burton, builders, 55 Garfield street
Jakeman Arthur, confectioner, 16 Ford End road
James John & Sons, tinplate workers, 11 Iddesleigh road
James Charles, clerk, 10 Sidney road
James John, tinplate worker, 4 Church street

Josselyn Lieut.-Col. Frederick John, chief constable, County police, Shire hall, St. Paul's square
Judge & Ball, plumbers, 11 Mill stret
Judkins Elizabeth Annie & Louisa Mary (Misses), preparatory school, 1 The Crescent
Juff John Fennell, baker, 62 & 64 Greyfriars walk
Juffs Wiliam Arthur, greengrocer, 51 Commercial road
Julian George, tailors' cutter, 5 Waterloo road
Juniper Emma (Miss), dressmaker, 23 Commercial road
Kapelle Louisa (Mrs.), milliner, 60 Iddesleigh road
Kasteleiner Joseph, Crown P.H. 1 Britannia road
Kaufmann Brothers, drapers, 49 Commercial road
Keech Arthur Richard, beer retailer, 29 Park road west
Keech Charles, boot maker, 59 Union street
Keech Isaac, beer retailer, 34 Tavistock street
Keech William, greengrocer, 62 Iddesleigh road
Keep Charles, Globe inn, 37 Ford End road
Kemp George, boot maker, 1 Dame Alice street
Kendall George, evangelist, Mizpah, Gladstone street
Kendall William Wheeler, umbrella manufacturer, 105 High st
Kenning Louisa (Mrs.),confectioner & beer retailer,12 Ampthill rd
Kennings Harry, boot & shoe maker, 19 Newnham street
Kent & Gostick, military boot makers, 84 High st. See advert
Kent Arthur George, baker, 7 Roise street
Kent Elinor Mary (Miss), teacher of music,.Milldown, Hurst gro
Kent Thomas Henry, baker, 18 Brace street
Killick Caleb, inland revenue officer & inspector of corn returns, 1A, St. Paul's square
Kilpin & Billson, wholesale, retail & furnishing ironmongers, iron merchants, cutlers, brass founders, tin, iron & zinc plate workers, braziers, coppersmiths, electric light & bell fitters & bell & gas fitters, hot water engineers, bath fitters, manufacturers of' the improved Bedford kitcheners, agents for the Phœnix Fire Insurance Office & Pelican Life Office, marble merchants & agricultural implement agents, 17 High street; workshops, Castle lane. Telegrams "Kilpin Billson, Bedford"; Telephone No. 7. See advertisement
Kilpin Charles, builder, 33 Prebend street
Kimber Alfred Herbert, coal dealer, 2 Beckett street
Kimbolton Avenue Lawn Tennis & Croquet Club, Kimbolton av
Kime John Henry, tailor & outfitter, 8 & 10 Silver street
King Arthur, draper, 20 & 22 St. Loyes street
King Edward, Bear inn, 92 High street
King Frank Ernest, cab proprietor, 23 Brereton road
King Harry, local agent for the Trevor & Wingfield estates, Rose cottage, Biddenham
King Henry St. John, baker, 35 Argyle street
King John, saddler & harness maker, 42 Tavistock street
King Sarah (Mrs.), householder, 31 Western street
King Sarah Elizabeth (Miss), apartments, 92 Castle road
Kingham Emily Kate (Mrs.), photographer, 7 Cauldwell street
Kingston Edwin William, tailor, 97 Tavistock street

During the early years of Queen Victoria's reign photographers were known as 'daguerreotype artists', named after Louis Daguerre who unveiled the first commercially viable photographic process in 1839. A database of early photographers can be searched at **www.earlyphotographers.org.uk** and there are also regional databases online like that at www.photolondon.org.uk. Find out more using the Royal Photographic Society's research guide at **www.rps.org/blogs/2013/september/researching-historical-photographers** and *My Ancestor was a Studio Photographer* by Robert Pols (2011).

All the fun of the fair

Not all photographers worked from a high street studio. Some were travelling tradespeople who captured couples and families enjoying a day out, and summer fairs proved the perfect opportunity. Lists of travelling photographers and operators of optical shows are available on the Travelling Show & Fairground Ancestors UK webpage at **www.members.shaw.ca/pauline777/TravellersUK.html**. It also contains rolls of showmen and other travellers extracted from records dating from 1851 to 1915.

Annual fairs have been held since royal charters were first granted during medieval times, sanctioning the public celebration of religious feast days, and many have their roots in ancient local customs. Itinerant fairground workers toured a local circuit throughout the calendar year, moving regularly from one parish to the next, and a variety of terms were applied to their roles. Travelling entertainers, amusement caterers, roundabout proprietors and market stall keepers all came under the remit of The Van Dwellers Protection Association established in 1889, now known as the Showmen's Guild of Great Britain (**www.showmensguild.co.uk**).

Travelling showmen consider the fair to be more than just a business. It became a way of life, and traditionally showmen took their whole family on the road. Charles Stock was described on his son's 1882 wedding certificate as a steam circus owner, setting a precedent for 6 generations of his descendants to follow. His great-x3-granddaughter is still in the business and immensely proud of her heritage.

The National Fairground Archive (NFA) at the University of Sheffield comprises extensive collections of family papers, posters, ephemera and photographs donated by showpeople. It has a complete set of the World's Fair newspaper back to 1904 and The Showman from 1900 to 1912. There is advice about researching fairground ancestors at www.sheffield.ac.uk/nfa/about/familyhistory and the archive's staff offer a professional research service for a fee (see **www.sheffield.ac.uk/nfa**). The definitive guide to 19th-century circus performers is J Turner's two-volume *Victorian Arena – The Performers: A Dictionary of British Circus Biography* (1995–2000) and includes thousands of biographies for clowns, acrobats and jugglers.

Musicians

The Worshipful Company of Musicians traces its history back 500 years. Thousands of pages of court minute books from 1772 to 1918 and other treasures have been digitised at **www.wcomarchive.org.uk**, and additional archives belonging to the Company can be accessed at the Guildhall Library (see **www.aim25.ac.uk/cats/118/14201.htm**).

Who's Who in Music, 1935, available on **TheGenealogist.co.uk**, covers a veritable mix of accomplished instrumentalists and vocalists, including the likes of Len George Harris who played the drums, banjo and trumpet and was in his own dance band that performed at the Grand Hotel in Brighton. Listed on the same page are singers from the Royal College of Music and Royal Military School of Music, the organist at St George's Chapel, Windsor Castle, and a school music teacher. The volume also contains a list of specialist newspapers and periodicals worth looking up at the British Library, like the *Accordion Times & Harmonica News*, and *The Organists Quarterly Record* containing "articles and news items of interest to players, students and builders of the organ". Incidentally, Birmingham Archives houses the British Organ Archive including records of many organ-building firms.

The Royal College of Music's database of London Music Trades at **http://lmt.rcm.ac.uk** covers composers, performers, publishers and instrument makers who were active in the capital between 1750 and 1800. The Royal College's archives, plus music collections held in around 600 other institutions, can be searched by musician's name at **www.cecilia-uk.org**. If your ancestor was a composer or had their recitals recorded then try searching the British Library's Music Collection (**www.bl.uk/subjects/music**) and Sound Archive (**www.bl.uk/subjects/sound**). These collections include recordings of songs by music hall legend Marie Lloyd.

Flamboyant music hall artistes commonly used stage names (Marie Lloyd was christened Matilda Alice Victoria Wood), so unless they were particularly successful they can be tricky to track down. Music halls rose to prominence in the late 19th century and continued to draw in crowds well into the 20th century with popular variety shows and comedy acts that appealed to the working class masses. The genre originated in the saloon bars of public houses but became so popular that purpose-built music hall auditoriums were constructed to accommodate larger audiences. Many of the sources recommended for researching theatrical ancestors are equally applicable to music hall performers.

Drinking holes

Alehouses have needed to be licensed since at least 1552 when victuallers started appearing before the Justice of the Peace to enter into a bond of recognizance promising that they would keep an orderly house. Quarter Sessions courts issued annual licences during so-called Brewster Sessions, and separate registers of alehouse keepers often survive in county record offices. As the name suggests, alehouses were kept by private householders who sold beer and ale, which might be home-brewed. Taverns traditionally sold wine and also needed to be licensed from the 16th century, while inns provided lodgings and often had a tavern attached where guests could dine. Purpose-built public houses as we know them began to appear from the early 19th century, and interiors became ever more sumptuous as the Victorian period progressed. By 1891 there were 78,000 publicans, innkeepers and hotel keepers in England and Wales.

Given that it was safer to drink alcohol than water in most towns before the late 19th century – and at one point it was acceptable for men, women and even children to partake of an alcoholic beverage during the working day – it is no shock that enjoyment often turned to excess and resulted in licences being revoked. Calendars of Worcestershire Quarter Sessions on **TheGenealogist.co.uk** are awash with indictments against people like husbandman Andrew Dallowe, accused of keeping an alehouse without a licence in 1609.

Intoxication invariably went hand-in-hand with the pursuit of illicit entertainment. Stringent laws against gambling were not relaxed until the mid 20th century, and court records and newspaper reports summarise offences committed by those who were caught engaging in and facilitating such illegal activities. In 1607 labourer John Haye of Anserwick was hauled before the Worcestershire Quarter Sessions for "allowing unlawful games to wit dancing in his house during Divine service and for lodging persons of ill fame".

One genealogist was astounded at the recent discovery that her own great-x3-grandfather was a beer and coal seller who kept "a house of infamous notoriety" in 1861. That last sordid detail was added to the census return by an enumerator who was in no doubt about the occupations of five young women boarding at the house, who are all plainly described as 'prostitutes'. Their brothel keeper was duly convicted later that same year at the Manchester Quarter Sessions. No town was free from vice, as Frances Finnegan discovered when she picked apart the lives of 1400 street walkers and brother keepers in her book *Poverty and Prostitution: A Study of Victorian Prostitutes in York* (1979), scrutinising the impact of the oldest profession in the world.

Quarter Sessions records can sometimes reveal the oldest profession

Chapter Seven:
Going Further

T his book has explored a range of occupations in turn, but there are certain resources that are useful for advancing your research into multiple professions, which we will look at in more detail here.

Original records

Maps are enormously useful for better understanding the nature of the area where your ancestors worked, whether they toiled in the fields or in the city. The collection of early Victorian tithe maps on **TheGenealogist.co.uk** was discussed in Chapter 1, as were even older enclosure maps, and we have touched upon the detailed Ordnance Survey maps produced regularly from the late 19th century that are found in local archive collections.

The National Archives has impressive cartographic collections, mostly attached to records of the government departments from which they originated. Therefore, if your ancestor had a military career, then map collections within the War Office series may illustrate fields of battle, and these can be complemented by additional collections held by the Imperial War Museum. Some government maps have been extracted from their original record series and are described at **www.nationalarchives.gov.uk/help-with-your-research/research-guides/maps-further-research/**. All should be found in the online catalogue at **http://discovery.nationalarchives.gov.uk**.

The National Archives' Colonial and Foreign Office series are also worth consulting for maps if your ancestor was posted abroad during the course of their work. The British Library has a collection of 4.5 million historical maps charting territory across the world, which are described at **www.bl.uk/subjects/maps**. The National Library of Wales (**www.llgc.org.uk/collections/learn-more/introduction3/**) also has mining maps, nautical charts and other cartographic treasures, and is one of the most important British map repositories along with the Bodleian Library in Oxford and Cambridge University Library, both of which are legal deposit libraries.

If your ancestors were rooted in the capital then explore Charles Booth's colour-coded 'poverty map' of London at http://phone.booth.lse.ac.uk to find out whether a shop or a business was situated in an affluent area of the city or on the fringe of a late-Victorian slum. Police notebooks for each district mention the types of tradespeople found on the streets, and name some of the local characters encountered by Booth's surveyors. His agents interviewed tailors, bootmakers, hatters and other workers during research for Booth's multi-volume *Life and Labour of the People in London* (1889–1903). Their notebooks record the operation of each trade in minute detail, and the originals can be read online at **http://booth.lse.ac.uk**. Booth's publication drew parallels between the population's working and living conditions and life expectancy. He noted that the death rate was particularly high in Shadwell and St George's in the East, probably owing to the exposed character of the riverside labour in these parishes.

If an ancestor died during the course of their work then the death certificate may indicate that an inquest was held. Coroners' inquests were reported in local papers including the *Illustrated London News* on **TheGenealogist.co.uk**, and provide great detail about the tasks that were carried out by the deceased in the lead-up to their death. An inquest held in 1842 on the body of William Winterbottom, a 52-year-old labourer at St Katherine's Docks, found that he worked in the bottling department. On the day of his death he went into several wine vaults to extinguish the lights. While shutting the trap doors behind him, he lost his balance and fell 18 feet into the cellar, fatally fracturing his skull. This may be the most detailed account available of his death and the nature of his work. There was never an obligation for coroners to keep records of inquests for longer than 15 years, however those that have survived will be found in the county record office.

Newspapers often provide the most graphic accounts of accidents and inquests, and as we have already seen they are a great source for adding colour to our ancestors' lives in all manner of ways. The National Library of Wales has an online database of both English and Welsh language papers dating from 1804 to 1919 at **http://newspapers.library.wales**. The British Library has the largest collection of newspapers from around Britain and the former British Empire, which can be accessed in a combination of digital, microfilm and original format at the News Room in St Pancras (**www.bl.uk/subjects/news-media**). To find a particular newspaper title, use the Advanced Search at **http://explore.bl.uk** and select 'Newspapers' from the list of material types (or select 'Journals' if you want to search for trade journals). The British Library's NEWSPLAN initiative encouraged local libraries to make available online catalogues of regional newspaper holdings, which can be found via **www.bl.uk/reshelp/bldept/news/newsplan/newsplan.html**.

DIG DEEP

Information about an ancestor's job can appear in the most unlikely of places – records of burials from the quarterly meeting of Bristol and Somerset Quakers, available to search in **TheGenealogist.co.uk**'s Nonconformist collection, include a printed slip dated 4 December 1776 instructing grave maker William Norris to dig a six-foot deep hole in the Friends' Burial Ground at Claverham for Mary Frampton who died the previous day. She was the 56-year-old widow of the late James Frampton, surgeon of Backwell in Somerset. The same slip confirms that Norris completed his duty and the body was buried two days later.

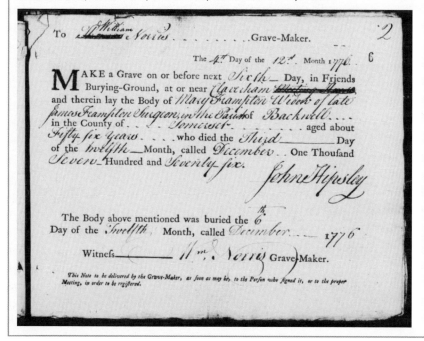

Regional collections

There are numerous finding aids for locating original records held in archives and university libraries across the country. The National Register of Archives has already been mentioned several times as being useful for tracking down the records of companies, organisations, families and prominent individuals. The electronic version of this register, along with the Access to Archives database that combines the online catalogues of hundreds of regional repositories, has recently been merged into The National Archives' Discovery catalogue http://discovery.nationalarchives.gov.uk. To make the most of this facility, use the Advanced Search and at the bottom of the page opt to 'Search other archives'. You can enter the name of a particular archive here, or instead press search and then use the filters in the side panel to refine the results from a number of archives.

Search for material held within higher education institutions, societies, livery companies and cultural organisations inside London at www.aim25.ac.uk. The scope of partner institutions is wide, from the Association of Anaesthetists to Transport for London's Corporate Archives. The records of many businesses and individuals are located by the database, and AIM25 also works closely with the Archives Hub, which provides a gateway to similar material held in over 220 institutions nationwide. The database at http://archiveshub.ac.uk scans document descriptions held in specialist collections like the Architectural Association Archives and the National Co-Operative Archive.

A combination of these catalogues should therefore be used to try to find archival material, but some individual record offices also maintain their own online catalogues. The National Archives' Archon directory at http://discovery.nationalarchives.gov.uk/find-an-archive provides contact details and web addresses for hundreds of UK archives. Search by region, town, or by keyword to find lesser-known places such as the Warner Textile Archive in Braintree.

Some regional organisations have collaborated with members of the public to digitise samples of locally held archive material and photographs in particular. Community websites like www.peoplescollection.wales celebrate the history of local industries using multi media, including oral history recordings. Staffordshire Past Track has over 25,000 items uploaded to www.staffspasttrack.org.uk. Using the Map Explorer to search for resources from Tamworth helps to locate a photograph of butcher Mr Redfern overseeing an ox roast with his assistant Billy Argyle during a special celebration in the town in 1913.

It's wonderful to find photographs of ancestors or even co-workers who lived in their neighbourhood, but we can also start to look for film footage of everyday scenes from the 1890s. Film makers Mitchell & Kenyon concentrated on 'actuality' during the Edwardian period, documenting ordinary street scenes. Many short clips were made of workers pouring out of factories, and these fascinating glimpses into the past can now be watched for free on the BFI Player online. Film archives all over the country have also collaborated, putting hundreds of regional films online. Footage depicting working life over the past hundred years can be found using the interactive map at **player.bfi.org.uk/britain-on-film/map/**, including an inspection of Manchester bobbies in 1901, and interviews with tradesmen and craftspeople around Bridport in 1951. Many of the participating archives are listed at **http://filmarchives.org.uk/join/members/** and hold additional film collections that haven't been digitised.

SNAPSHOTS OF THE PAST

The Image Archive on **TheGenealogist.co.uk** consists of thousands of old photographs depicting working life, including women employed in a can factory, nurses in a maternity ward in the 1930s, and car assembly lines. Places of employment are also documented, with photographs of many street scenes and prominent buildings. The shop fronts of Julius Southon & Son and Chapman's Stores are clearly visible in a photograph of Balham High Road from the first decade of the 20th century. Using immersive 3D technology a cotton-winder at a lace factory in Nottingham is brought to life in a WiggleGram. Colour and black-and-white photos can be searched by place name or by keyword at **www.thegenealogist.co.uk/imagearchive/**.

Detailed guides

The works of numerous authors who have written lengthy guides to certain aspects of employment history have been noted in this book. Mark Herber's tome *Ancestral Trails* (2008) contains an enormous amount of information about researching our ancestors' occupations, and it can be browsed online page-by-page in the Reference Books section of **TheGenealogist.co.uk**. In particular, see Chapter 22 for additional records of trades, professions and businesses.

If you want to expand your knowledge of a specific old trade then check out the catalogue of books published by the Society of Genealogists, the Federation of Family History Societies and Pen and Sword, which focus on industries and occupations associated with particular regions, and the minutiae of individual professions, such as Stuart A Raymond's *Surrey and Sussex Occupations: A Genealogical Guide* (2001) and Ian Waller's book *My Ancestor was a Leather Worker* (2015). The WorldCat database at **www.worldcat.org** identifies the locations of two billion books held in 10,000 libraries worldwide.

Concise research guides put together by various archives have also been suggested in previous chapters, including many by The National Archives. Its in-depth guides cover a mammoth assortment of subjects, far more than have been mentioned in this book. To find out if there is a guide to your area of interest, go to **www.nationalarchives.gov.uk/help-with-your-research/#find-a-research-guide**. Here you can search by theme, browse an A to Z list, or search for all relevant tutorials using the keyword search box.

The National Archives also has a series of interesting podcasts recorded from educational talks that are held regularly at Kew. The catalogue of over 300 lectures can be listened to online at **http://media.nationalarchives.gov.uk** and includes many valuable tips for researching people who worked in the Army, Navy, Merchant Service, Secret Service, Colonial Office, as well as general advice for using business archives and overcoming brick walls.

Get hands on

Visiting museums related to your ancestors' occupations helps to answer questions about their experiences that aren't readily explained in archive documents. Many museums can be found using the Archon directory at **http://discovery.nationalarchives.gov.uk/find-an-archive**, which provides links to places like Quarry Bank run by the National Trust in Wilmslow. This water-powered cotton mill built in 1784 has been restored and is open to the public alongside an Apprentice House where pauper children who worked in the mill slept. The steam engines and old machinery continue to clatter and whir, recreating the sounds that were familiar to the mill workers over a hundred years ago. Visit Britain also offers inspiration for days out on its heritage pages at **www.visitbritain.com** and the most comprehensive guide to museums and heritage sites around the UK (plus archives and family history societies), *The History & Heritage Handbook*, is available via **www.heritagehunter.co.uk/DYA**.

The Weald and Downland open-air museum celebrating rural life in the South East of England has a popular programme of courses where you can try your hand at your ancestor's profession. There are butchery lessons, introductions to coppice management and ploughing with heavy horses, wool spinning classes and practical sessions on ancient carpentry techniques, building flint walls and thatching. You can book courses online at **www.wealddown.co.uk/learn/**.

Heritage courses around the country can be found at **www.hotcourses.com** and on the website of the National Heritage Training Group at **www.the-nhtg.org.uk/training-quals/training-course-provider-search/** including brickwork, lime plastering and blacksmithing courses should you consider really getting back to your roots and following your ancestor's trade as a career!

Why not try your ancestor's trade?

Bibliography

Nick Barratt, *Who Do You Think You Are? Encyclopedia of Genealogy* (HarperCollins, 2008)

Joyce Culling, *Occupations: A Preliminary List* (FFHS, 1999)

Mark Herber, *Ancestral Trails* (Sutton, 2004)

Andrew Jewell, *Crafts, Trades and Industries: A Book List for Local Historians* (NCSS, 1968)

Stuart Raymond, *Occupational Sources for Genealogists* (FFHS, 1996)

Stuart Raymond, *Trades and Professions: The Family Historian's Guide* (Family History Partnership, 2011)

The National Archives, *Records Of British Business and Industry 1760–1914* (HMSO, 1990–1994)

Margaret Ward, *Female Occupations: Women's Employment 1850–1950* (Countryside Books, 2008)

Colin Waters, *A Dictionary Of Old Trades, Titles And Occupations* (Countryside Books, 2002)